VICTORIAN
BRICK AND TERRA-COTTA
ARCHITECTURE
in Full Color

---
160 PLATES

Edited by
PIERRE CHABAT

Dover Publications, Inc.
NEW YORK

Copyright © 1989 by Dover Publications, Inc.
All rights reserved under Pan American and International
Copyright Conventions.

Published in Canada by General Publishing Company, Ltd.,
30 Lesmill Road, Don Mills, Toronto, Ontario.
Published in the United Kingdom by Constable and Company, Ltd.

This Dover edition, first published in 1989, reproduces all the plates from the two
portfolios (of 80 plates each) titled *La Brique et la Terre Cuite* (Series I published by
V[euv]e A. Morel et Cie, Paris, 1881; Series II, by Librairies-Imprimeries Réunies [ancienne
maison Morel], Paris, n.d. [not earlier than 1889]). See Publisher's Note for further
details. The Publisher's Note and captions, based on the original French text, were newly
prepared for the present edition, as was the Glossary of French Terms.

Manufactured in the United States of America
Dover Publications, Inc., 31 East 2nd Street, Mineola, N.Y. 11501

Library of Congress Cataloging-in-Publication Data

Brique et la terre cuite. English.
Victorian brick and terra-cotta architecture in full color /
edited by Pierre Chabat.
p.   cm.
Reproduces all the plates from the two portfolios titled La Brique
et la terre-cuite published in Paris by various publishers, 1881–ca. 1889.
ISBN 0-486-26164-6
1. Building, Brick. 2. Building, Terra-cotta. 3. Architecture, Victorian.
I. Chabat, Pierre, 1827–1892. II. Title.
NA4120.B7513   1989
721'.04421'09034—dc20   89-17141
CIP

PUBLISHER'S NOTE

As the Victorian arts, once decried, are subjected to an ever more intense reevaluation, architecture emerges as one of the supreme accomplishments of the era. In our own Postmodernist day, eclectic ornamentation is no longer perceived as a vice, and we now long for touches of color in our streetscape. The Victorians often achieved bold color effects by using bright appliqués of terra-cotta and by the imaginative use of brickwork—a construction technique in which patterning (the various "bonds") is an inescapable corollary of the need for stability. Other than the surviving buildings themselves (not always free of later alterations or industrial grime), a monumental contemporary and authentic visual record still remains to us in a now exceedingly rare and valuable set of portfolios, Pierre Chabat's *La Brique et la Terre Cuite,* in which a large and varied array of constructions of the 1870s and 1880s are illustrated in the pristine splendor of their color.

Chabat (1827–1892) was a French architect who worked for a major railroad before becoming a municipal architect in Paris in 1865. By the time he published the first series (80 plates) of *La Brique et la Terre Cuite* (Brick and Terra-Cotta) in 1881, he was also a teacher of architecture and construction at two major institutions and the author of several reference works in the field. The subtitle of this first series, which Chabat edited in association with the architect Félix Monmory, was *Etude historique de l'emploi de ces matériaux; fabrication et usages; motifs de construction et de décoration choisis dans l'architecture des différents peuples* (Historical study of the use of these materials; their manufacture and modes of use; motifs of construction and decoration selected from the architecture of various nations). This expensive publishing project must have been a success, because less than ten years later (about 1889) the same firm issued the second series of 80 plates (edited by Chabat alone), which bore the subtitle: *Seconde série comprenant: Villas, hôtels, maisons de campagne, lycées, écoles, églises, gares, halles à marchandise, abris, écuries, remises, pigeonniers, cheminées, etc.* (Second series, including: villas, town houses, country homes, high schools, elementary schools, churches, railroad stations, covered markets, shelters, stables, sheds, pigeon houses, chimneys, etc.).

Other types of buildings covered by the two series include restaurants, hospitals, shelters for domestic and zoo animals, a gymnasium, a slaughterhouse and a number of structures for three Parisian world's fairs (1867, 1878 and 1889), which were always showcases for innovation and experiment. The wide variety of buildings ranges from the highly decorative to the more severe, from every type of Victorian revival ("Neo") style to muscularly functional structures that point beyond H. H. Richardson and into the early twentieth century. In addition to the many buildings—and the invaluable floor plans provided in many cases—several plates are devoted to patterns, motifs and details, occasionally derived from examples of architecture antedating the Victorian era but still operative as inspiration.

Most of the buildings and patterns illustrated are from France, but there is also material from Belgium, Holland, Germany, England and Italy. Only a handful of plates show unrealized designs; the overwhelming majority depict actual buildings, some of which are standing today. Many of the architects and builders have been forgotten, but there are such important practitioners as Davioud and Auguste-Joseph Magne, not to mention Alexandre-Gustave Eiffel, whose wrought-iron tower erected for a Parisian world's fair became an honored centenarian in 1989.

The long text issued with the first series includes a survey (now out-of-date) of brick construction from earliest times and a description of how bricks and tiles were manufactured in France in Chabat's day. Disappointingly, this text states almost nothing about the rationale, spirit or practice of architecture in the Victorian era itself. On the other hand, the "Explanation of the Plates" that accompanies both series supplies isolated bits of specific information on technology, materials and costs. (None of the text has been retained in the present edition, although some data from the "Explanation of the Plates" have been incorporated into the new English captions.)

As Chabat himself was the first to acknowledge, the breathtaking plates are the heart of the publication, and they are all reproduced in full color here. Originally numbered I through LXXX in each series, they have been given a through numbering here (1–160) for convenience of reference. The typography beneath each plate in the original edition consisted of: the name of Chabat (in Series I, also of Monmory) as project director, the name of the publisher (for this, see the Dover copyright statement, opposite), the name of the printer (Imprimerie Lemercier, Paris), the name of the lithographer (and sometimes other artist) responsible for the given plate, and a brief caption to the plate, usually including identification of the architect. In the present edition, the names of the lithographers appear only in a separate alphabetical list, whereas the architects continue to be credited in the captions as well as in an alphabetical list. The new English captions supplement the material from the French captions with other material from the "Explanation of the Plates," supply fuller names for some of the architects and add some geographical data to help locate the towns referred to.

The French typography within the color area of the plates could not be readily eliminated or replaced. It has been retained, but a complete French-English glossary of terms has been provided. The scale printed on most of the plates is in the form "scale of . . . to a meter." It should be noted that in the present edition the plates have had to be reduced (variously, but by an average of 18%), so this must be taken into account in any calculations.

Alphabetical List of Architects, Builders and Decorators

(The numbers are those of the plates.)

Amanovich, J.: 121.
Auburtin, E.-M.: 104–106.
Baudot, A. de: 70, 114.
Baumier: 119, 120, 136, 145.
Blondel, H.: 138.
Bonnier: 126, 127.
Bouvard, J.: 153, 154.
Breney: 138.
Brunnarius: 137.
Buysschaert: 8.
Cantagrel: 21.
Chabat, Pierre: 34, 55, 77, 79, 85, 98, 99, 108, 143, 144.
Chabat, Pierre, & E. Degand: 156.
Chipiez, Charles: 132, 135, 142.
Cléry: 71.
Dartein, de: 56–58.
Darvant, A.: 100, 101.
Davioud, Gabriel-Jean-Antoine: 67.
Déchard, Paul: 110.
Delarue: 141, 149.
Deslignières: 49–52.
Dutert, Ferdinand: 150.
Eiffel, Alexandre-Gustave: 69.
Erard, H.: 89.
Feine, A.: 91, 131.
Formigé: 158, 159.
Guadet: 40.
Guérinot: 111, 112.
Hédin, A.: 102.
Héret: 90.
Hügelin: 157.
Jamaer, V.: 62, 63, 86.
Jandelle-Ramier, E.: 122, 123.
Janvier: 23, 24.
Joachim: 37, 44.

Jory: 130.
Laisné, C.: 30.
Langlais: 20.
Lecoq & Delanoye: 96.
Lereculeur: 41.
Lethorel, L.: 115.
Lewicki, Edouard: 134.
Lheureux: 109.
Lisch, J.: 27, 33, 128, 129.
Macé, Eugène: 53, 54, 100, 101, 107.
Magne, Auguste-Joseph: 64.
Magne, Lucien: 81–84.
Marin, F.: 117.
Massy, Robert de: 133.
Mennessier: 75.
Moyaux, C.: 65, 66.
Mussigmann: 97.
Papinot, E.: 92.
Parent, Henri: 76.
Questel, C.: 46–48.
Roussel, A.: 68.
Saintin, E.: 152.
Sauvestre, S.: 43, 69.
Scellier de Gisors: 160.
Sédille, Paul: 116, 124, 146–148.
Simonet: 25, 26, 31, 32, 35, 36, 95, 155.
Tronquois: 87, 88.
Van Heukelum: 42.
Vaudremer, E.: 74.
Verheul, J.: 125.
Wable: 59.
Wilkinson, J. Starke: 61.
Winders, J. J.: 60.
Wulliam & Farges: 139, 140.

Alphabetical List of Artists

(The numbers are those of the plates. The artists whose names are followed by a single asterisk are credited with the original drawing of the respective plates; those with two asterisks, with the engraving of the plates. All others are credited with the lithographing of the plates. "F. Penel" is possibly just an error for "J. Penel.")

Arnaud*: 45.
Bénard: 134, 135, 154.
Brandin: 7, 41.
Châtaignon: 1, 6, 11, 14, 29, 42, 47, 65, 55, 79.
Coin: 28, 30, 33–36, 43, 50–52, 56–58, 60–64, 69–78, 80, 86, 93, 96, 97, 100, 101, 107, 114–116, 118, 121–123, 128, 129, 136, 139, 141, 142, 145, 148–150, 155.
Courtois: 2–5, 8, 18, 22, 45, 49, 53, 54, 68.
Daumont: 87, 88, 104–106, 110, 124, 132.
Devienne, A.*: 26.
Dousselin: 108.
Massot: 9, 10, 19, 48.
Méheux: 109.
Ollé: 32, 37.

Penel, F.**: 126.
Penel, J.**: 83, 84, 89, 97, 127.
Petitgrand, V.*: 31.
Regamey, F.: 27.
Sanier: 23, 39, 55.
Schmidt: 59.
Spiégel: 13, 15–17, 20, 21, 24, 25, 38, 44, 46, 81–85, 89, 90, 92, 94, 95, 98, 99, 102, 103, 111, 112, 117, 119, 120, 125–127, 130, 131, 137, 140, 143, 144, 146, 147, 151, 153, 156–160.
Storck, J.**: 25, 31.
Thurwanger: 91, 113, 133, 138, 152.
Valez, J.*: 28.
Werner: 12, 40, 67.

Glossary of French Terms on the Plates

abreuvoir: watering trough
abside: apse
angle, d': (at the) corner, angle
antichambre: anteroom
architecte: architect
armoire: closet
arr[ondissemen]t: administrative division of Paris
atelier: studio
atelier salon: studio-parlor
au dessous de: below
Autriche-Hongrie: Austro-Hungarian Empire
axe: axis
baie: bay
bains: bathroom
balcon: balcony
basse-cour: farmyard
bâtiment des malades: building for patients
bibliothèque: library
bouveries: cattle stalls
box(e): (horse) box
buanderie: laundry room
bureau: office
cab[ine]t d'aisances: toilet
cabinet de toilette: dressing room
cabinet de travail: study
calorifère: heating unit
cave (à bois): (wood) cellar
caveau: small cellar; understair closet
ch[ambre]: room
chambre à coucher: bedroom
chambre d'ami: guest room
chambre de domestique: servant's room
chambre d'enfant: child's room, nursery
chambre d'isolement: isolation room
chapelle: chapel
charbon: coal
charbonnier: coal cellar
chef du dépôt: depot master
cheminée: chimney
chéneau: gutter
citerne: cistern
classe: class
combles: roofing
commun(e): common
concierge: janitor, gatekeeper, porter
corniche: cornice
côté: side
coupe: section
cour (de service): (service) courtyard
courette: small courtyard
couronnement: capping
couvert(e): covered
cuisine: kitchen
de: of
déb[arr]as: storage room
dégagement: private passage
dépendances: outbuildings; annexes; service buildings
dépôt: depot; engine shed
des: of the

dessin: drawing
détail: detail
deuxième (2ᵉ) étage: third floor; two flights up
dortoir: dormitory
droit: right
du: of the
échaudoir: scalding room
ech[elle] de . . . p[our] m[ètre]: scale of . . . to a meter (the numbers are expressed in fractions of m[eters] and in c[entimeters])
école communale: elementary school
école maternelle: nursery school
écurie: stable
élévation: elevation
employé: employee, clerk
entrée: entrance
escalier: staircase
été: summer
études: preparation rooms
façade, face: facade
faïencier: earthenware maker
fait(e): made
fenêtres: windows
filles: girls
fontaine: fountain
forge: forge
fosse: cesspool
fosse mobile: portable latrine
frise: frieze
fumier: manure
fusils: rifles
galerie: gallery, passage
garçons: boys
garde-manger: pantry
général(e): general
glacière: ice house
grand: big
grenier: garret
gymnase: gymnasium
habitation: dwelling, residence
hauteur, à la: at the level (of)
hôtel des monnaies: mint
infirmerie: infirmary; sick bay
intérieur(e): interior
jardin: garden
jardinet: small garden
jeunes filles: girls
la: the
lampisterie: lamp room
lapinières: rabbit warrens
latéral(e): lateral, side
lavabo: lavatory
laverie: laundry
le, les: the
légende: legend
lingerie: linen room
linge sale: soiled linen
loge: porter's or gatekeeper's lodge
logement: lodging, apartment

longitudinal(e): longitudinal
mécanicien: engineer
mer: sea
monte-plats: dumbwaiter
mur de clôture: enclosing wall, party wall
nettoyage: cleaning; refuse
office: pantry; servant's hall
orangerie: orangery
palier: landing
parloir: visiting room
passage: gangway
pavillon: pavilion
perron: perron, front steps
perspectif, perspective: (in) perspective (plan)
petit: small
pharmacie: pharmacy
pigeonnier: pigeon house
pignon: gable (end)
plan: plan, view, section
plan retourné: cross section looking upward
porche: porch
porte (charretière): (carriage) gate
poste d'eau: water connection
postérieur(e): back, rear
poulailler: chicken coop
préau couvert: covered playground
premier (1er) étage: second floor; one flight up
principal(e): chief, main
réfectoire: refectory, lunchroom
remise: shed; engine shed
réservoir: tank
resserre: toolshed
rez-de-chaussée: ground floor, first floor, street level
rue: street

S[ain]te-Barbe: Saint Barbara
salle à manger: dining room
salle de bain: bathroom
salle de billard: billiards room
salle des gens: servants' room
salle d'exercices: exercise room
salle d'observations: observation room
salon: salon, parlor, living room
séchoir: drying room
second étage: third floor; two flights up
sellerie: saddle room, harness room
serre: greenhouse
sous-sol: basement
Suisse: Switzerland
supérieur(e): upper
sur: on, onto
terrasse: terrace
terre-plein: earthern terrace, raised ground
tisan(n)erie: patients' kitchen
transept: transept
transversal(e): cross, transversal
travée: bay
trou à fumier: manure pit
Union Céramique: Ceramic Union
véranda: veranda
vestibule: vestibule
ville: city
vins fins: vintage wines
vins ordinaires: dinner wines
vitré(ed): glazed
voitures: carriages
vue: view
W.C.: toilet

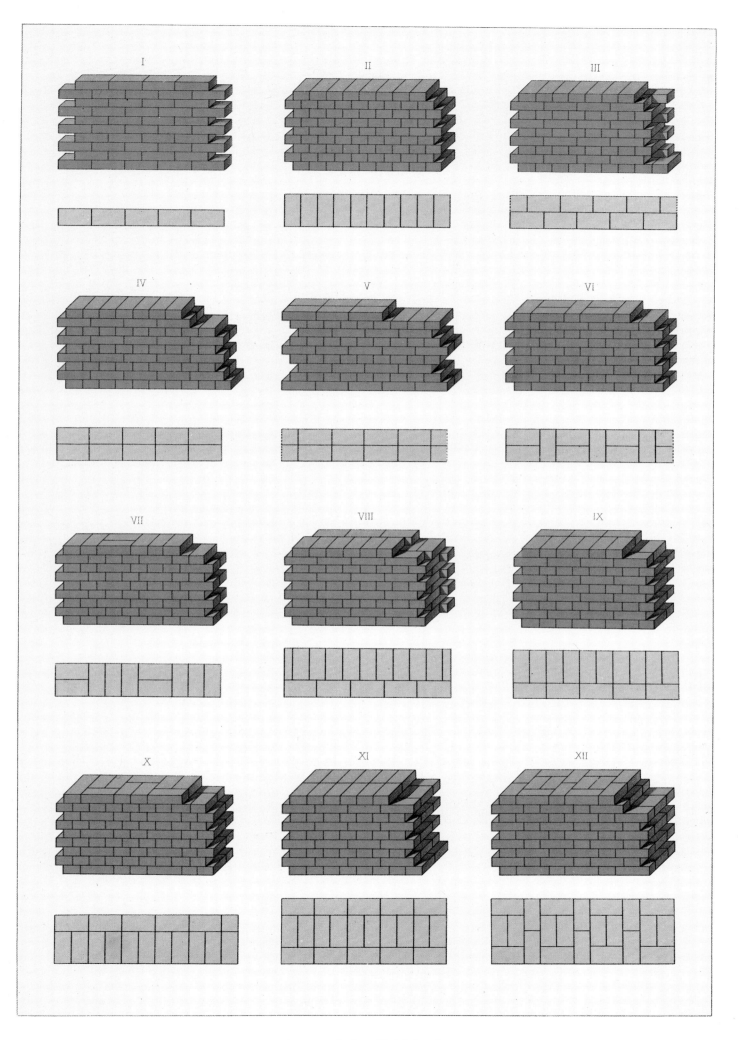

PLATE 1: Styles of brick bonds.

PLATE 2: Tile patterns (based on the paving of Amiens cathedral).

PLATE 3: Tile patterns (based on the paving of Amiens cathedral).

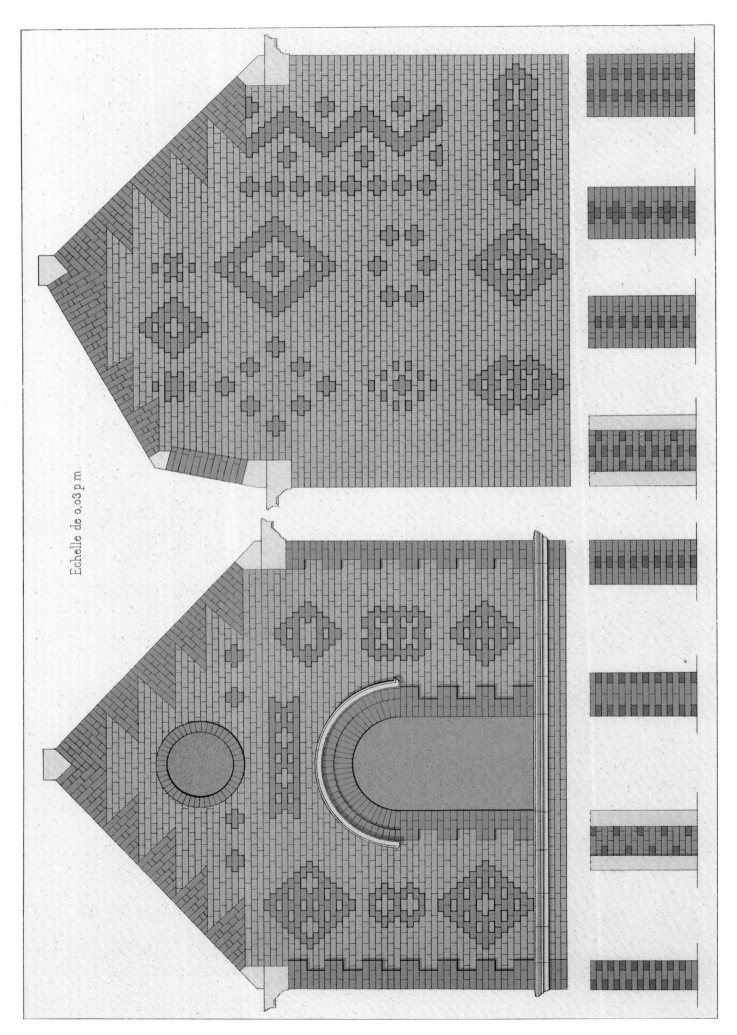

Echelle de 0,03 p.m.

PLATE 4: Gable ends and piers typical of northern France.

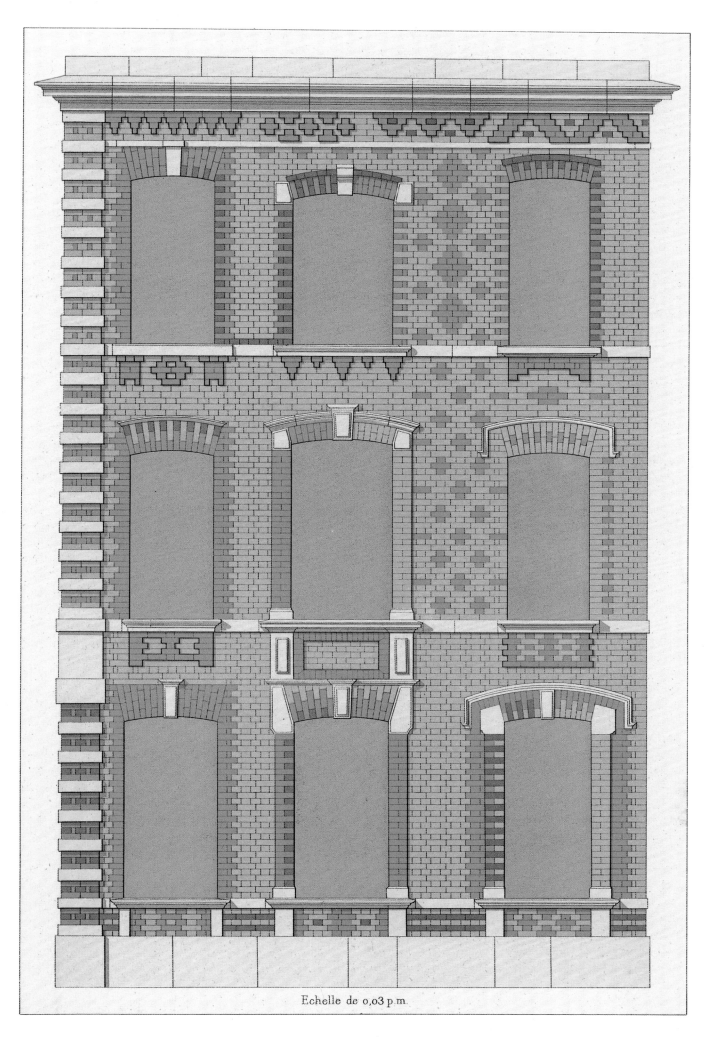

Echelle de 0,03 p.m.

PLATE 5: Windows.

Echelle de 0,025 pour mètre

PLATE 6: Brick patterns in the Château d'Anet (1548; Eure-et-Loir *département*).

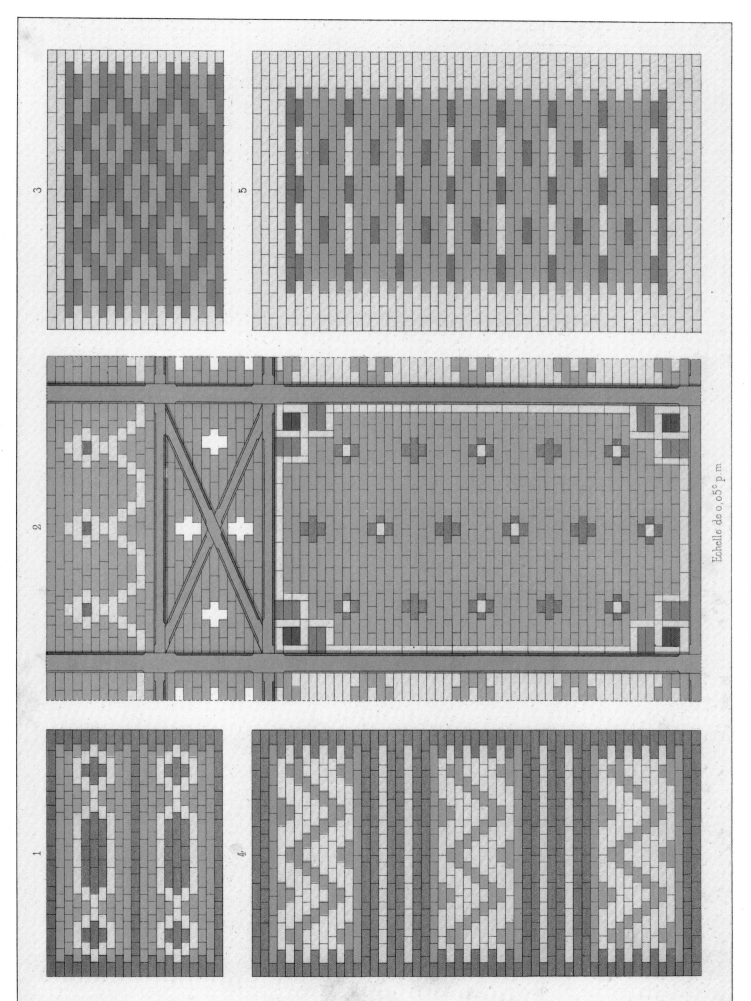

Echelle de o,o5ᶜ p.m

PLATE 7: Brick panels, from pavilions at the Exposition Universelle (World's Fair, Paris) of 1878.

1

2

3

Echelle de 0,04 p m.

PLATE 8: Window cappings from a house in Brussels; architect: Buysschaert.

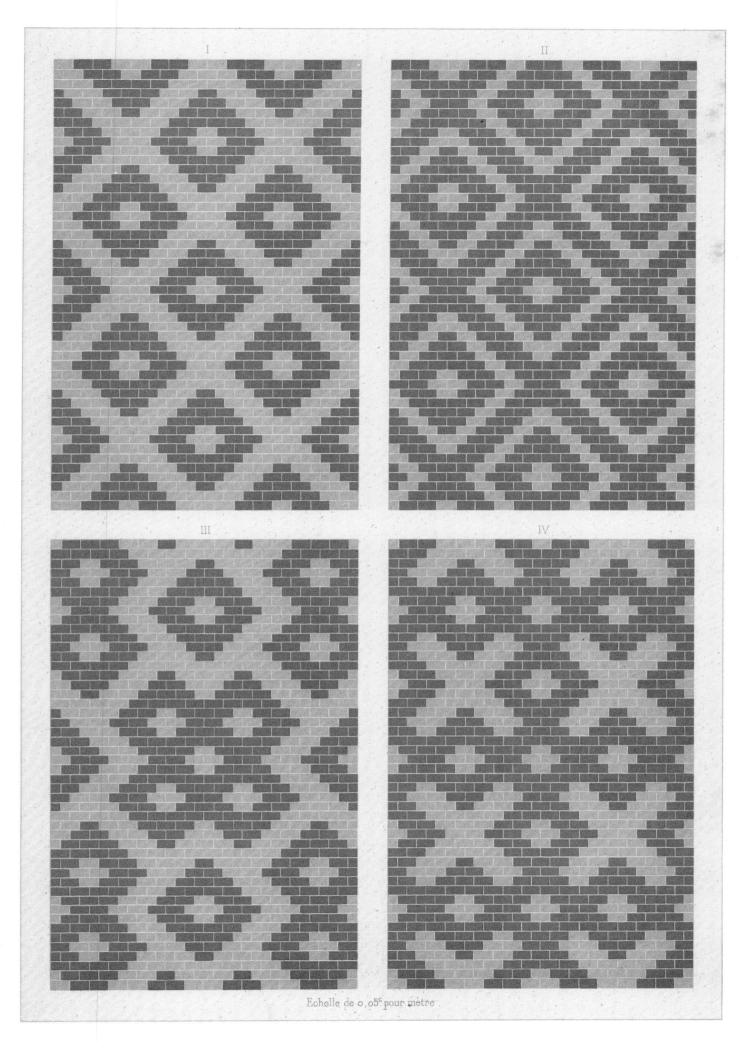

I   II

III   IV

Echelle de o ,o5ᶜ pour mètre

PLATE 9: Patterns for uninterrupted walls.

Echelle de o,o5ᶜ pour mètre

PLATE 10: Patterns for uninterrupted walls.

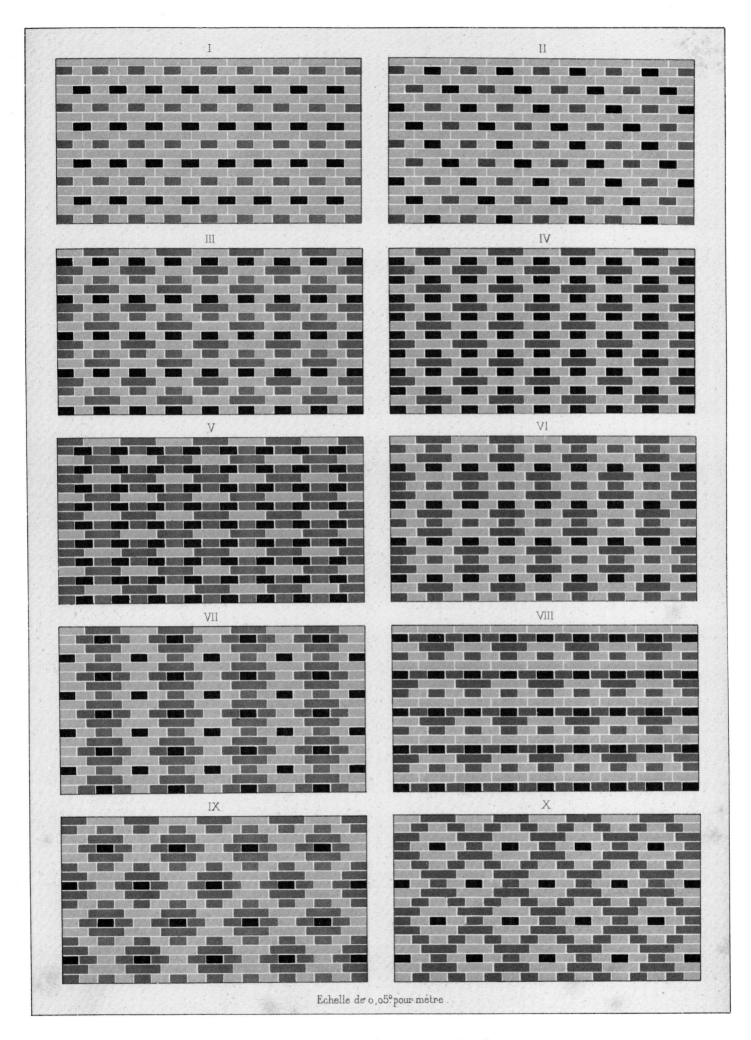

Echelle de 0,05º pour mètre.

PLATE 11: Patterns for uninterrupted walls.

Echelle de 0,04ᶜ p.m. ——————— Echelle de 0,10ᶜ p.m.

PLATE 12: Terra-cotta balustrades, from models displayed at the Exposition Universelle of 1878.

PLATE 13: Openwork in walls.

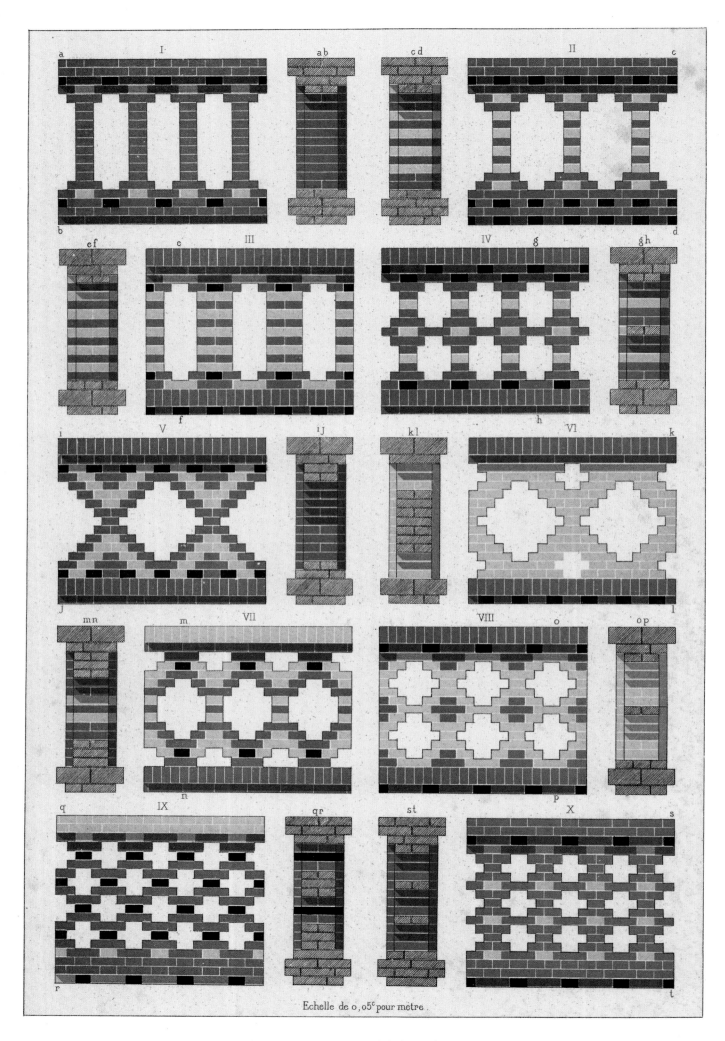

PLATE 14: Openwork balustrades.

PLATE 15: Ten terra-cotta tile patterns.

PLATE 16: Openwork in walls, from Tuscany and the former Papal States.

PLATE 17: Archivolts (arch moldings), from Rome.

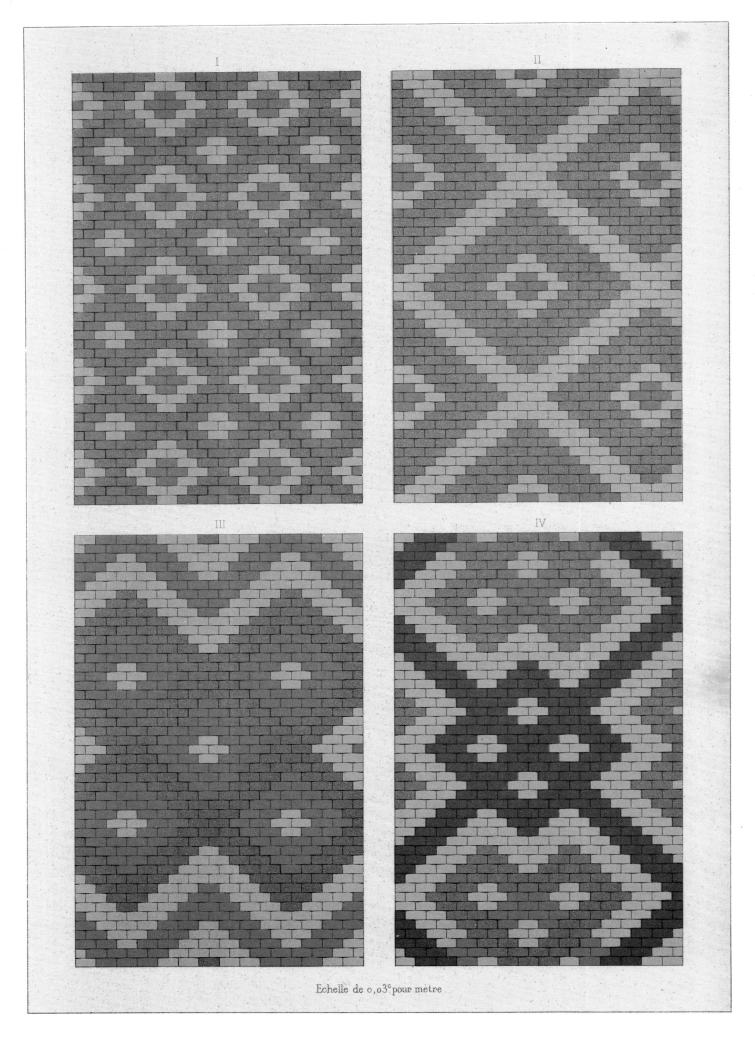

I

II

III

IV

Echelle de 0,03° pour mètre

PLATE 18: Four patterns for glazed tile roofing, from old French buildings.

I

II

III

Echelle de 0,02^c pour mètre

PLATE 19: Cladding of basements of three different Parisian markets.

Plan retourne E F

Plan retourne G H

E   F

G   H

A   B

C   D

Plan A B

Plan C D

Echelle de 0,10c p.m.

PLATE 20: Chimney shafts at the Lisieux station, Cherbourg line; architect: Langlais.

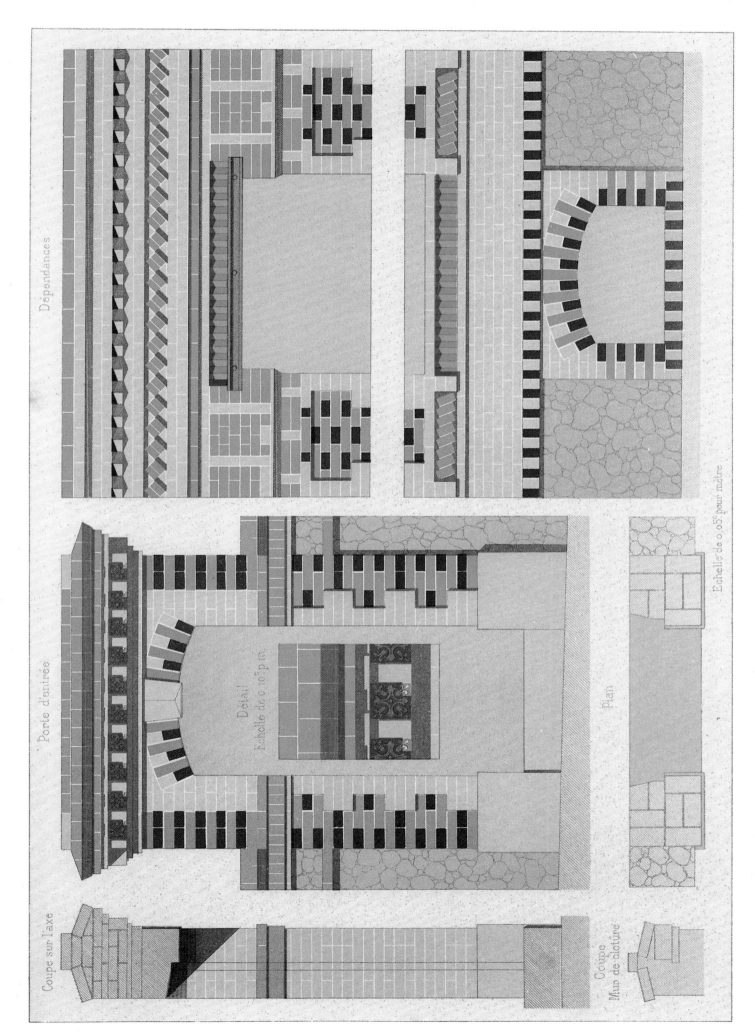

Dépendances

Porte d'entrée

Coupe sur l'axe

Coupe
Mur de clôture

Détail
Échelle de 0.10ᵐ p.m.

Plan

Échelle de 0.05ᵐ pour mètre

PLATE 21: House in Sèvres (Paris); architect: Cantagrel.

PLATE 22: Windows.

Echelle de o,o5ᶜ pour mètre.

PLATE 23: Window in the restaurant of the abattoir of La Villette (Paris); architect: Janvier.

Echelle de 0,04ᶜ pour mètre.

Echelle de 0,10ᶜ pour mètre.

PLATE 24: Gable of the refreshment bar, abattoir of La Villette; architect: Janvier.

Elévation

Echelle de 0,025 pour mètre.

PLATE 25: Rabbit house, Bois de Boulogne zoo (Paris); architect: Simonet.

Détail
face intérieure

Echelle de 0,05ᵉ pour mètre

PLATE 26: Rabbit house, Bois de Boulogne zoo (Paris); architect: Simonet.

PLATE 27: Champ de Mars railroad station, Exposition Universelle, 1878; architect: J. Lisch.

Echelle de 0.04 pour mètre

Couronnement de fenêtre
Rez-de-Chaussée
Echelle de 0,10ᵉ p m.

A

B

C

0,05 p.m.

PLATE 28: House in Berlaimont (Nord *département*).

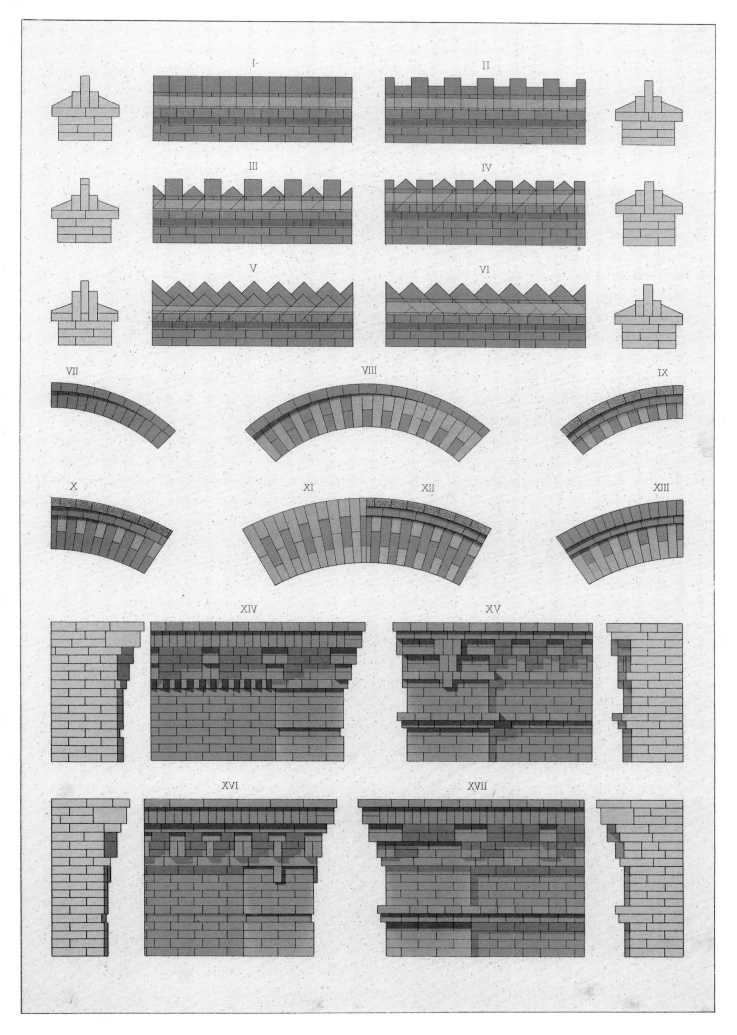

PLATE 29: Capstones, arches and cornices, from western France.

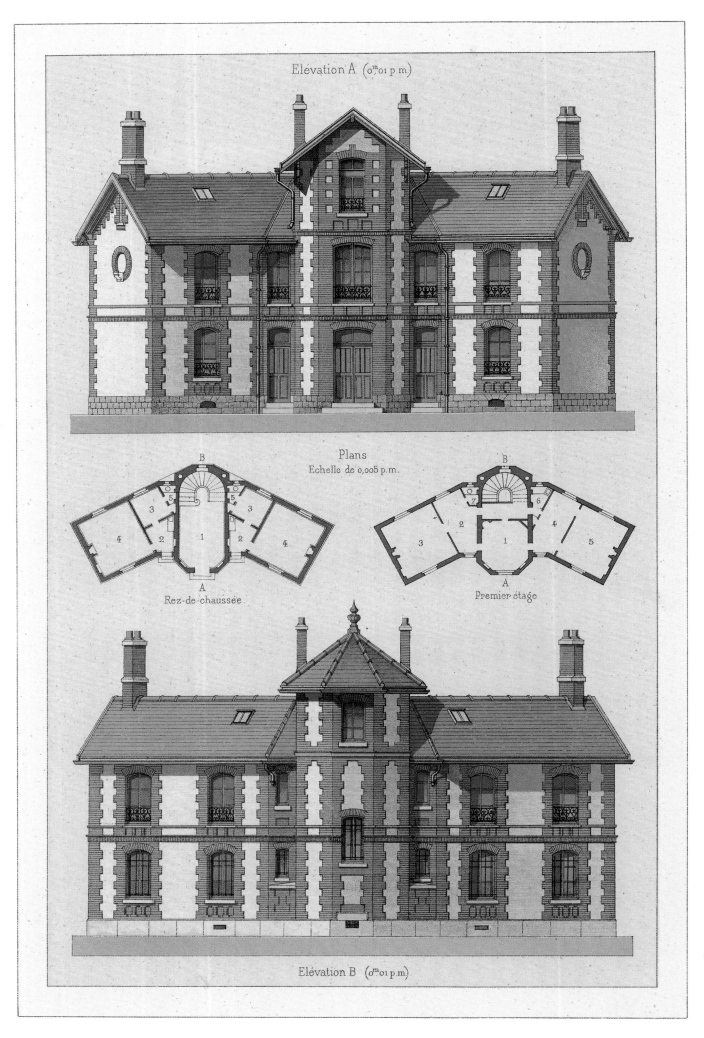

Elévation A (0ᵐ01 p.m)

Plans
Echelle de 0,005 p.m.

B

5   3
    2
4   1   2
                3
                    4

A
Rez-de-chaussée.

B

7   6
2   4
3   1   5

A
Premier étage

Elévation B (0ᵐ01 p.m)

PLATE 30: Gardeners' house, National School of Pharmacy, Paris; architect: C. Laisné.

Elévation.

Echelle de 0,01ᵉ pour mètre

A Face principale _ B Face postérieure

PLATE 31: Dovecote, Bois de Boulogne zoo (Paris); architect: Simonet.

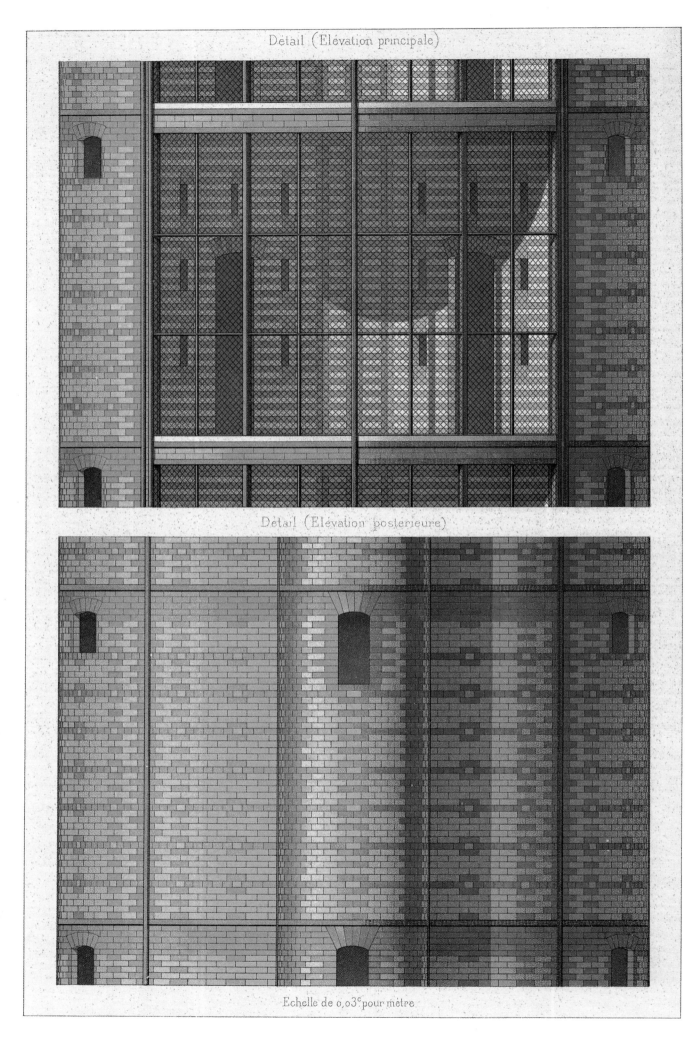

Détail (Elévation principale)

Détail (Elévation postérieure)

Echelle de 0,03ᶜ pour mètre

PLATE 32: Dovecote, Bois de Boulogne zoo (Paris); architect: Simonet.

Elévation principale

Elévation postérieure

Echelle de 0,015 pour metre

PLATE 33: Refreshment room, Champ de Mars station, Exposition of 1878; architect: J. Lisch.

Elévation

Coupe

Echelle de 0,025 p.m.

PLATE 34: Factory, rue Notre-Dame-des-Champs, Paris; architect: Pierre Chabat.

Elévation latérale
o^m o15 p^m

Plans

1er Etage

Rez-de-chaussée

Combles

Echelle de o,oo5 p^m

PLATE 35: House in Maurecourt (Seine-et-Oise *département*); architect: Simonet.

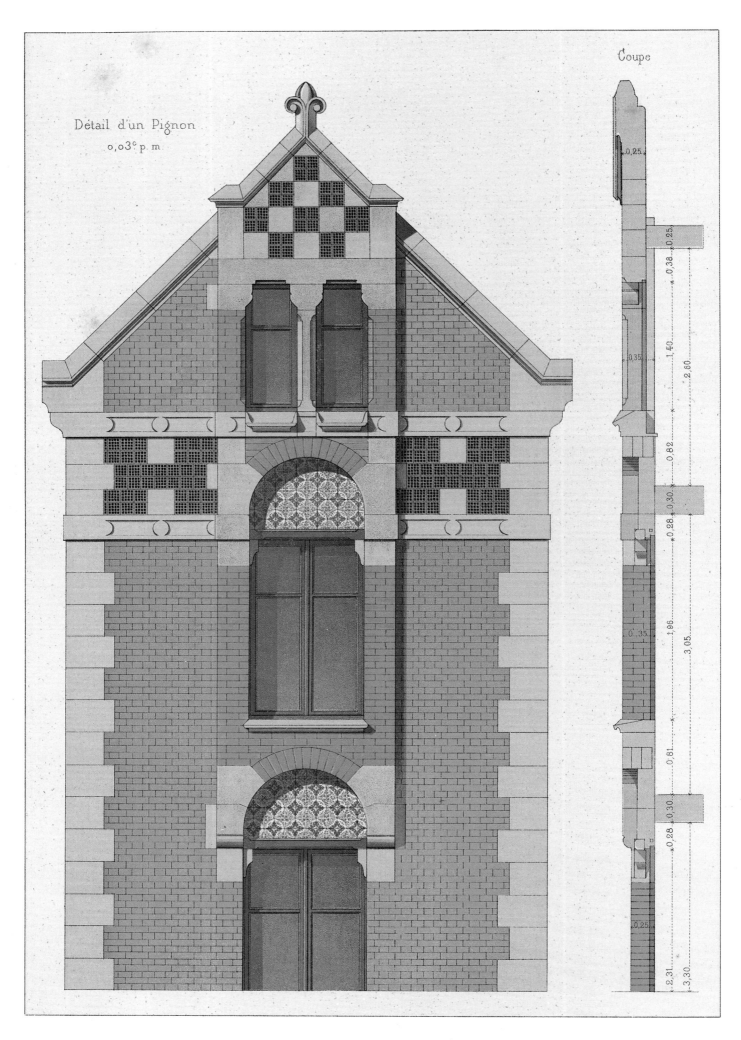

Détail d'un Pignon

0,03° p. m.

Coupe

PLATE 36: House in Maurecourt; architect: Simonet.

Elévation principale.

Elévation postérieure

Echelle de 0,02 pour mètre

PLATE 37: Exhibition shed intended for the Exposition Universelle of 1878; builder: Joachim.

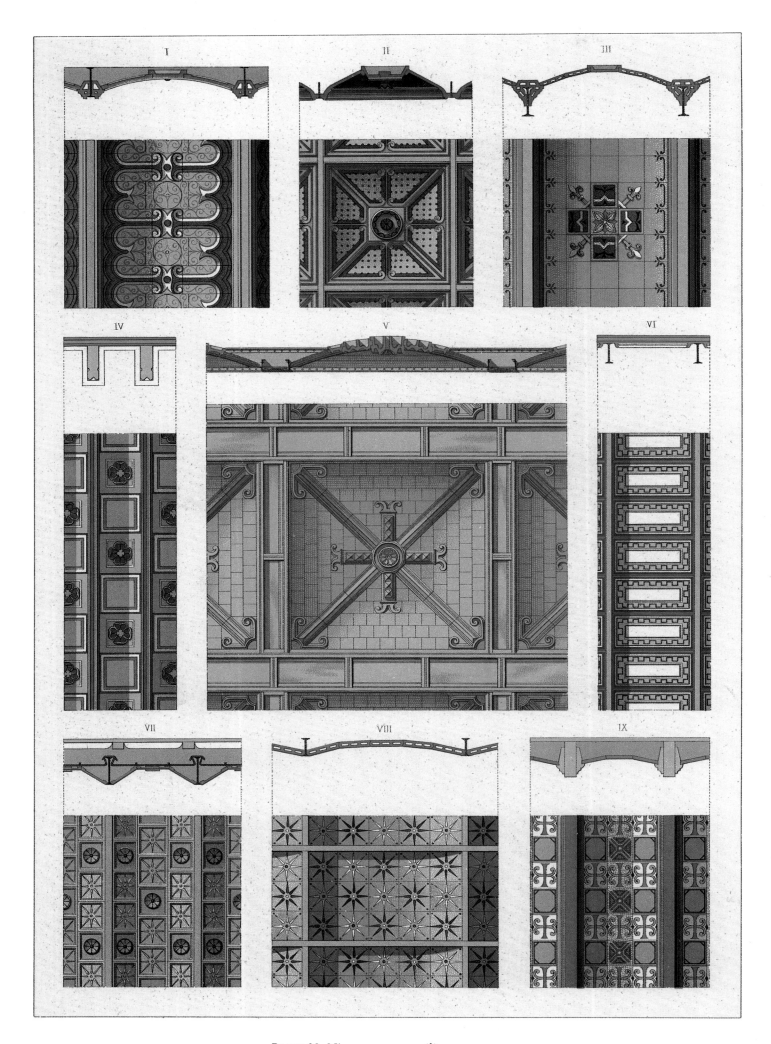

PLATE 38: Nine terra-cotta ceiling patterns.

Echelle de 0,01 pour mètre.

PLATE 39: Small railroad station near Munich.

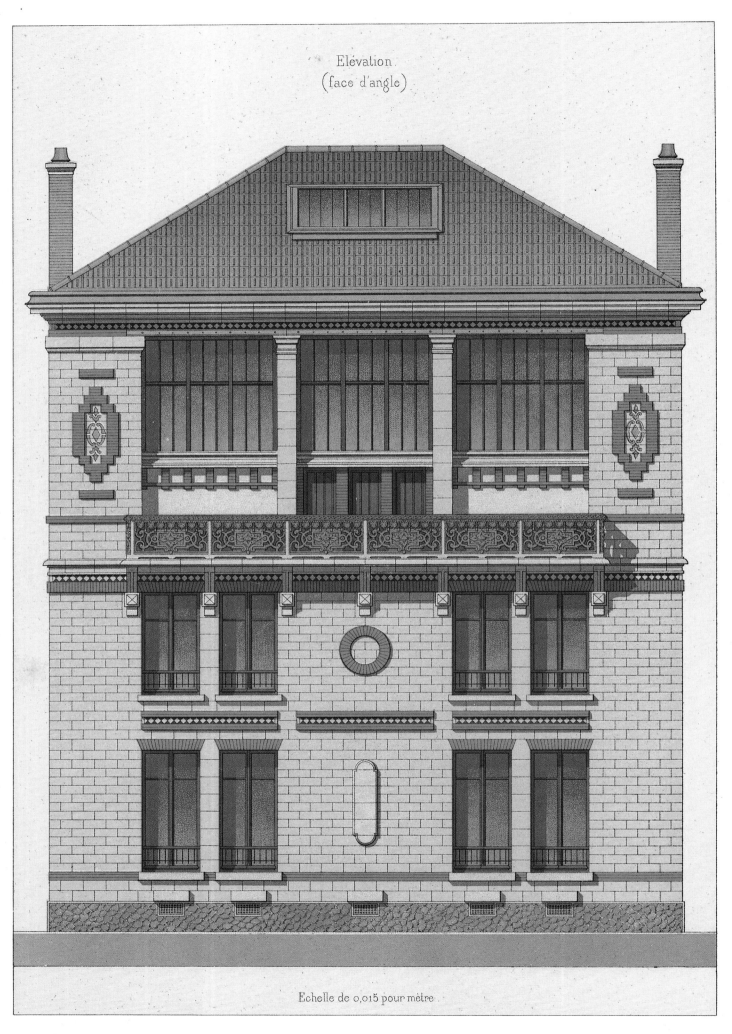

Élévation.
(face d'angle)

Echelle de 0,015 pour mètre.

PLATE 40: Painter's house, avenue Duquesne, Paris; architect: J. Guadet.

Pignon
Echelle de 0,015 p.m

Élevation

Plan du Rez-de-Chaussée

Détail de la Corniche

Plan du Grenier

0,005 p.m

0,05 p.m

0,005 p.m

PLATE **41**: Farmer's house, Cherouvillers (Eure *département*); architect: Lereculeur.

Echelle de 0^m.05^c pour mètre.

PLATE 42: Porch in Dutch style, Exposition Universelle of 1878; builder: N. Van Heukelum.

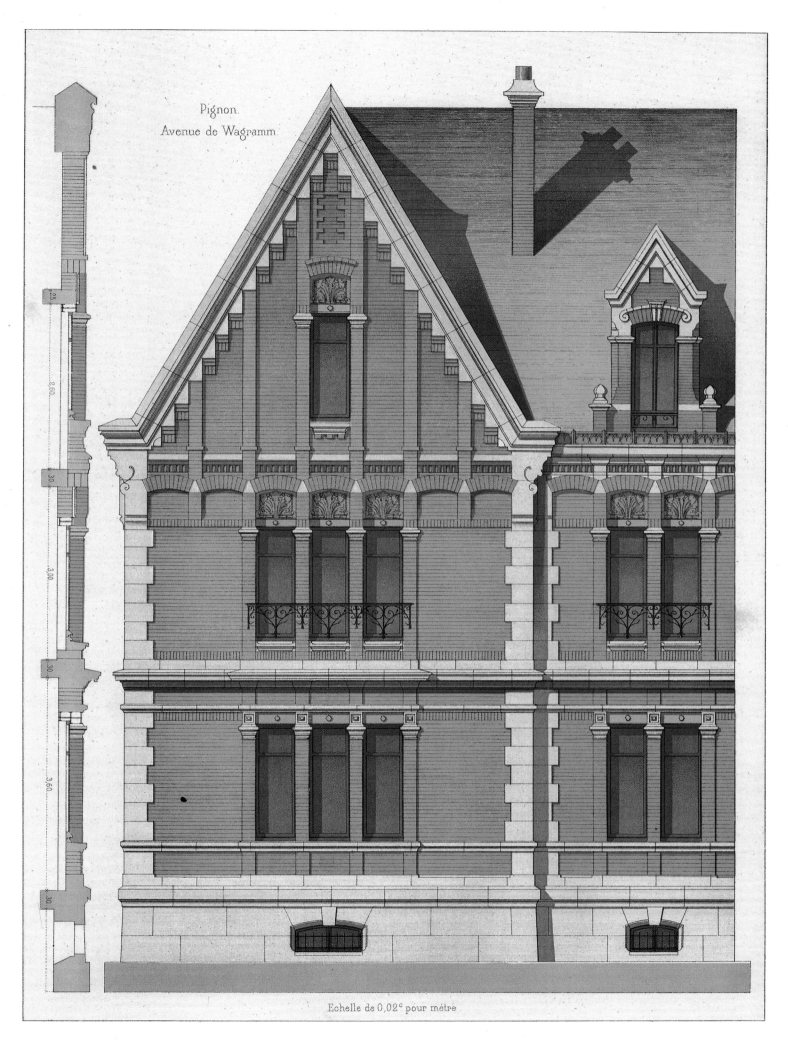

Pignon.
Avenue de Wagramm.

25.
2.60
30
3.00
30
3.60
30

Echelle de 0,02ᶜ pour mètre

PLATE 43: Town house, Paris; architect: S. Sauvestre.

Autriche-Hongrie
0,005 p.m.

Détails
0ᵐ.02 p.m.

Suisse
0,005 p.m.

Plan

0ᵐ.01 p.m.

Plan

0ᵐ.01 p.m.

PLATE 44: Factory smokestacks, Exposition Universelle of 1878; builder: Joachim.

I

II

Echelle de 0,25 pour mètre

PLATE 45: Tile patterns by the English firm Minton displayed at the Exposition Universelle of 1867.

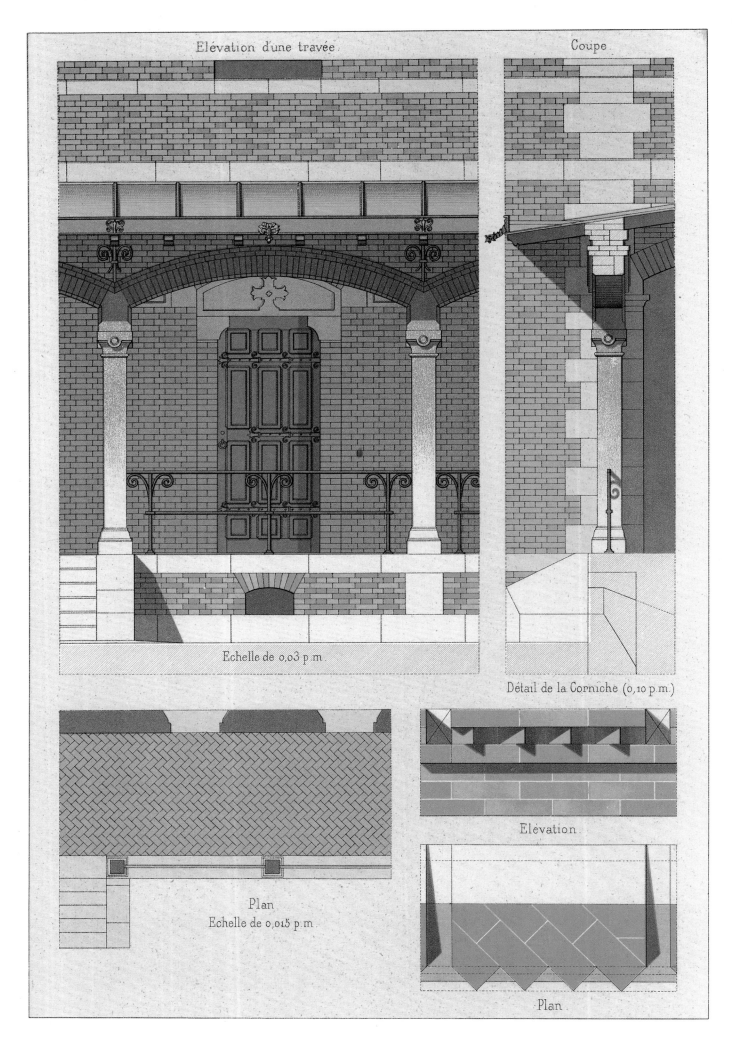

Elévation d'une travée

Coupe

Echelle de 0,03 p.m.

Détail de la Corniche (0,10 p.m.)

Plan
Echelle de 0,015 p.m.

Elévation.

Plan.

PLATE 46: Portico, hospital of Gisors (Eure *département*); architect: C. Questel.

Élévation

Coupe

Échelle de 0,02c pour mètre.

PLATE 47: Main building on the courtyard, hospital of Gisors; architect: C. Questel.

Bâtiment des malades.
0ᵐ.02ᶜ.p.m.

Chapelle.
(Face principale)
0ᵐ.02ᶜ.p.m.

PLATE 48: Gables, hospital of Gisors; architect: C. Questel.

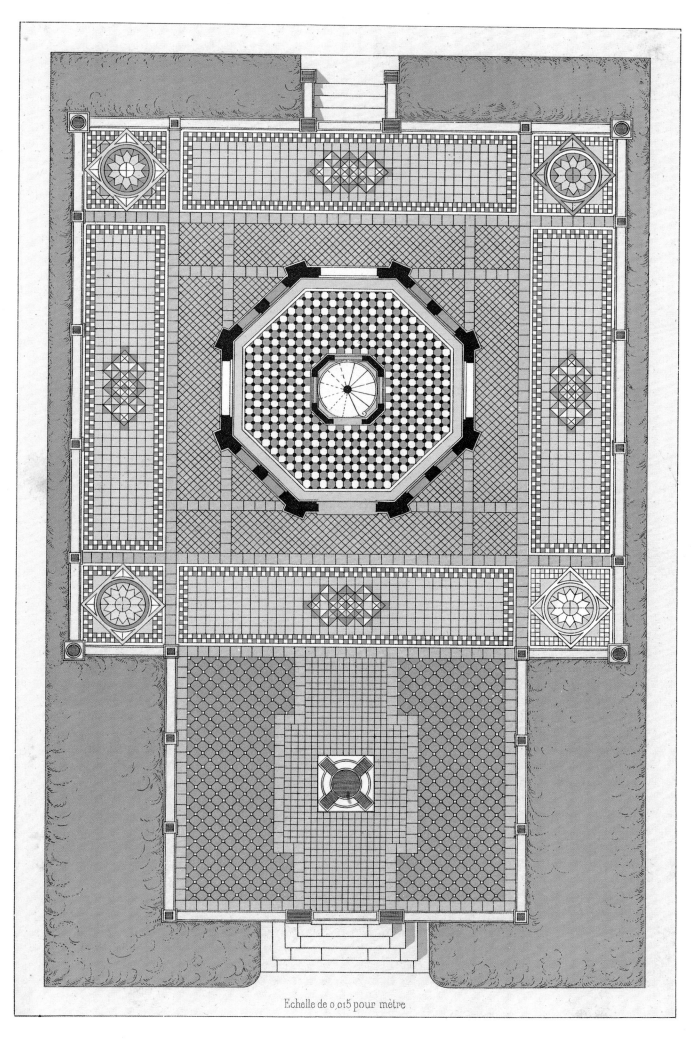

Echelle de 0,015 pour mètre

PLATE 49: Ceramics pavilion, Exposition Universelle of 1878; architect: Deslignières.

UNION CÉRAMIQ
UNION CÉRAMIQUE
Echelle de 0,015 pour mètre.

PLATE 50: Ceramics pavilion, Exposition Universelle of 1878; architect: Deslignières.

PLATE 51: Ceramics pavilion, Exposition Universelle of 1878; architect: Deslignières.

PLATE 52: Ceramics pavilion, Exposition Universelle of 1878; architect: Deslignières.

2

Élévation A

Détails 0,03 p.m.

1er Étage.

Echelle 0,02 p.m.

1

3

Rez-de-chaussée.

Plans 0,005 p.m.

PLATE 53: Stable and storage shed, Villers-sur-Mer (Calvados *département*); architect: Eugène Macé.

Elévation C

Elévation B

Echelle de 0,02 p.m.

PLATE 54: Stable and storage shed, Villers-sur-Mer (Calvados *département*); architect: Eugène Macé.

Détail Perspectif

Coupe

Face latérale

$0^m05\,p\,m$

PLATE 55: Gardener's house at Bagneux (Paris); architect: Pierre Chabat.

PLATE 56: Ministry of Works building, 1878 Paris fair (also Philadelphia, 1876); architect: de Dartein.

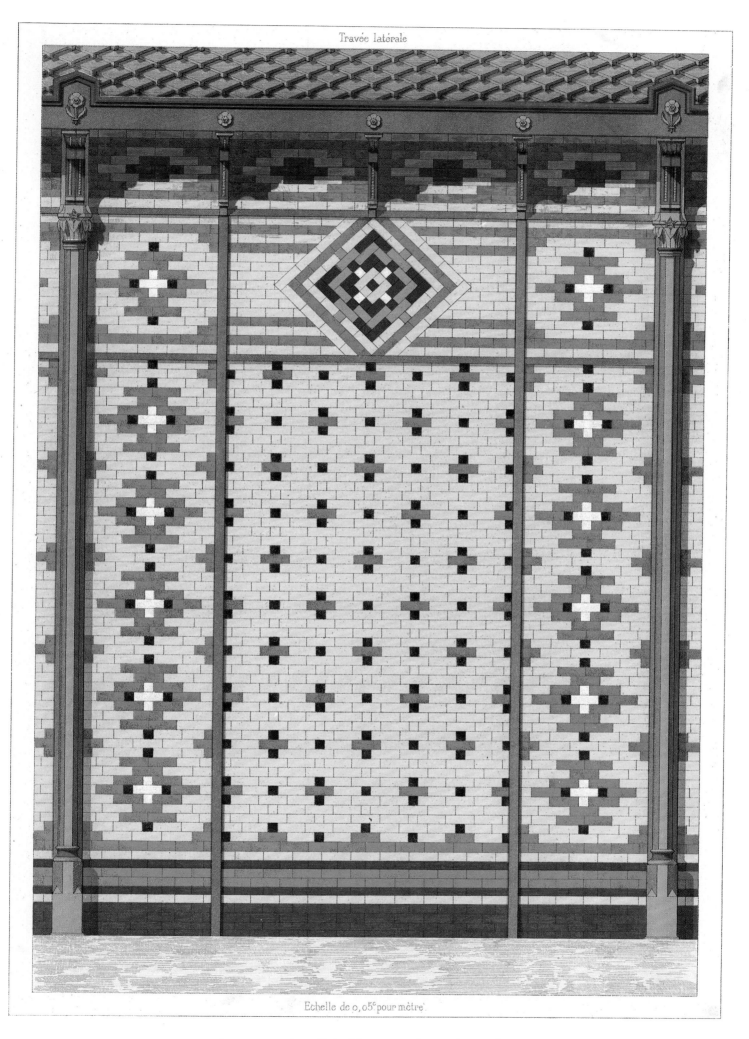

Travée latérale

Echelle de 0,05° pour mètre.

PLATE 57: Ministry of Works building, 1878 fair; architect: de Dartein.

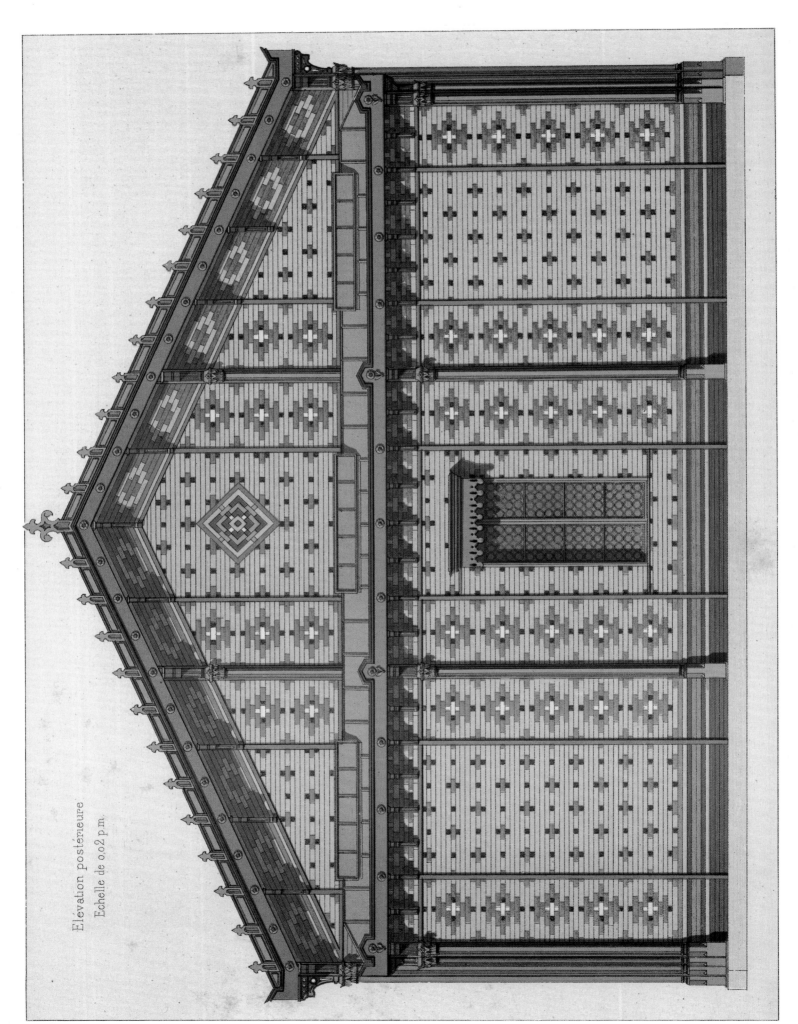

Élévation postérieure
Echelle de 0,02 p.m.

PLATE 58: Ministry of Works building, 1878 fair; architect: de Dartein.

Echelle de 0,025 pour mètre

PLATE 59: Algerian palace, Exposition Universelle of 1878; architect: Wable.

Élévation.
Ech. de 0,015 p.m.

Coupe

M. PAUWELS

PLATE 60: Pauwels workshop, rue de la Vigne, Antwerp; architect: J. J. Winders.

Echelle de 0,025 pour mètre.

PLATE 61: Doulton building, Exposition Universelle, 1878 (based on original in Lambeth); architect: J. Starke Wilkinson.

PLATE 62: Two lower stories of a house in Brussels; architect: V. Jamaer.

PLATE 63: Two upper stories of a house in Brussels; architect: V. Jamaer.

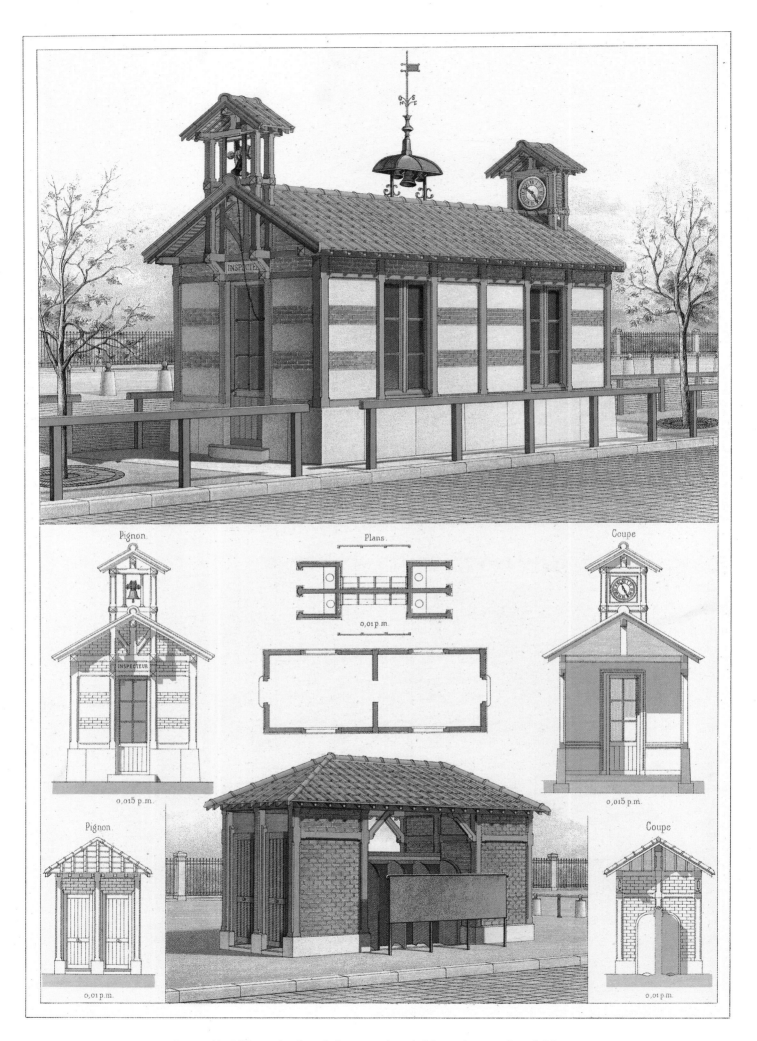

Pignon

Plans.

0,01 p.m.

Coupe

INSPECTEUR

0,015 p.m.

0,015 p.m.

Pignon

Coupe

0,01 p.m.

0,01 p.m.

PLATE 64: Office and toilet of a horse market; architect: Auguste-Joseph Magne.

Plan A B

o.o1. p m

Plan C D.

o.o1. p m

Echelle de o^mo4^c pour mètre.

PLATE 65: Church in Nœux-les-Mines (Pas-de-Calais *département*); architect: C. Moyaux.

C   D

1877

A   B

S.ᵗᵉ BARBE

Échelle de 0ᵐo4ᶜ pour mètre

PLATE 66: Church in Nœux-les-Mines; architect: C. Moyaux.

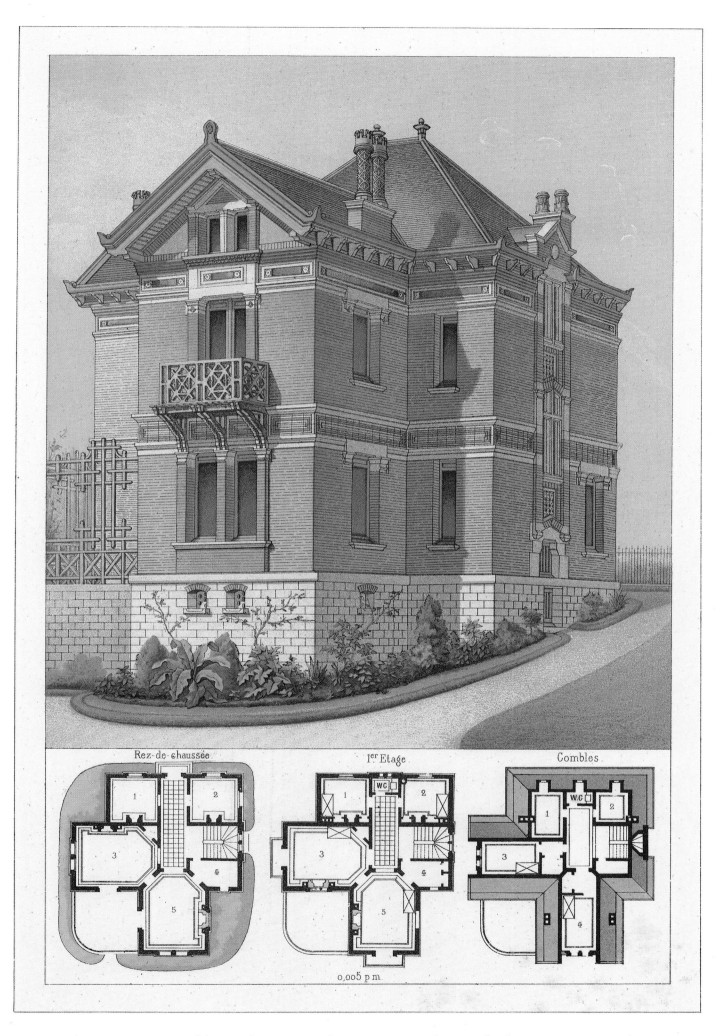

Rez-de-chaussée   1er Etage.   Combles.

0,005 p.m.

PLATE 67: Former park keepers' house, Buttes Chaumont (Paris); architect: Gabriel-Jean-Antoine Davioud.

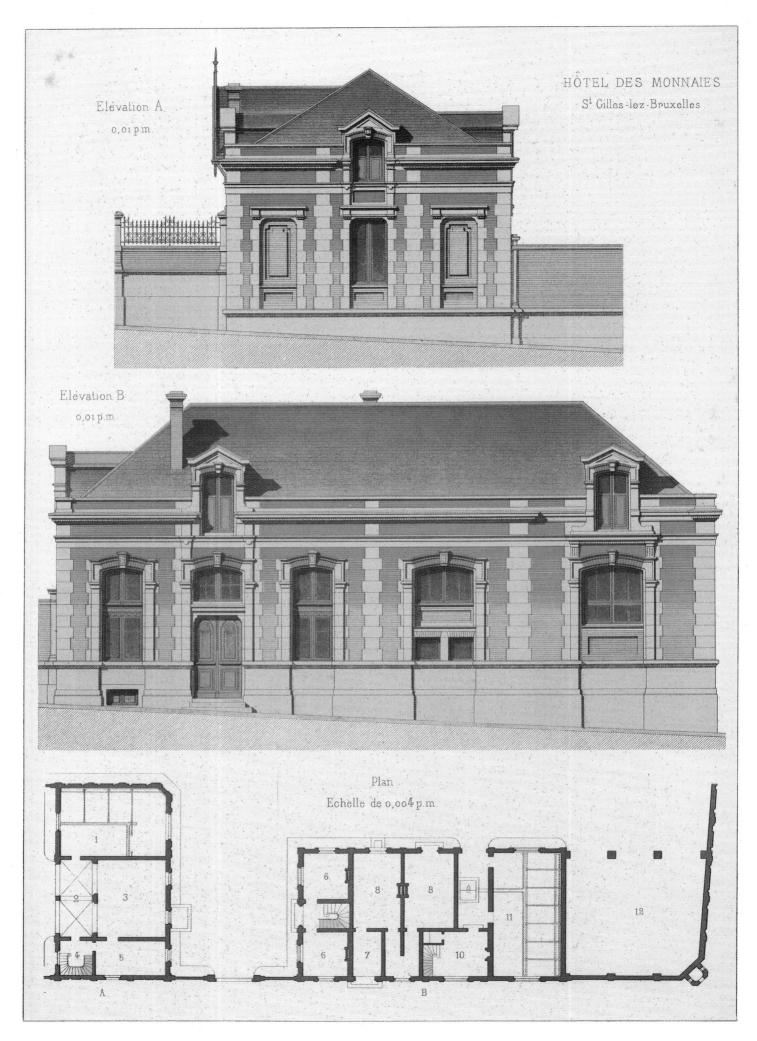

Elévation A
0,01 p.m.

HÔTEL DES MONNAIES
St Gilles-lez-Bruxelles

Elévation B
0,01 p.m.

Plan
Echelle de 0,004 p.m.

PLATE 68: Service buildings of the Brussels mint; architect: A. Roussel.

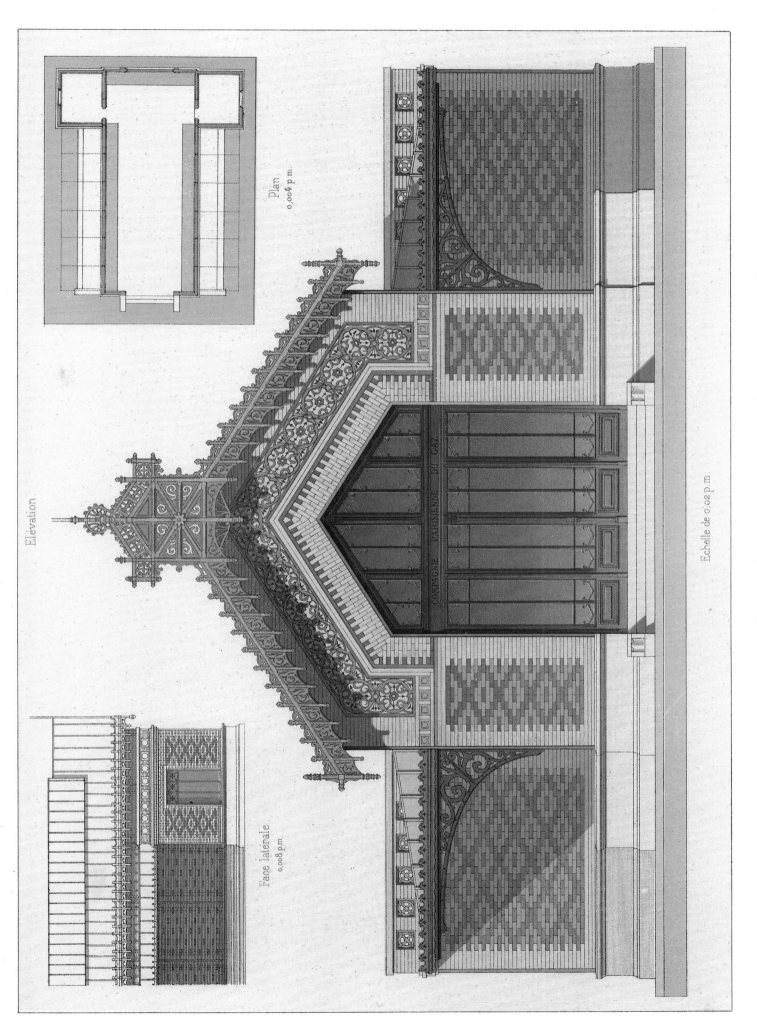

Plan.
o,oo4 p.m.

Elévation.

Face latérale.
o,oo8 p.m.

COMPAGNIE PARISIENNE DU GAZ

Echelle de o,o2 p.m.

PLATE 69: Paris gas company pavilion, 1878 fair; architect: S. Sauvestre; builder: Alexandre-Gustave Eiffel.

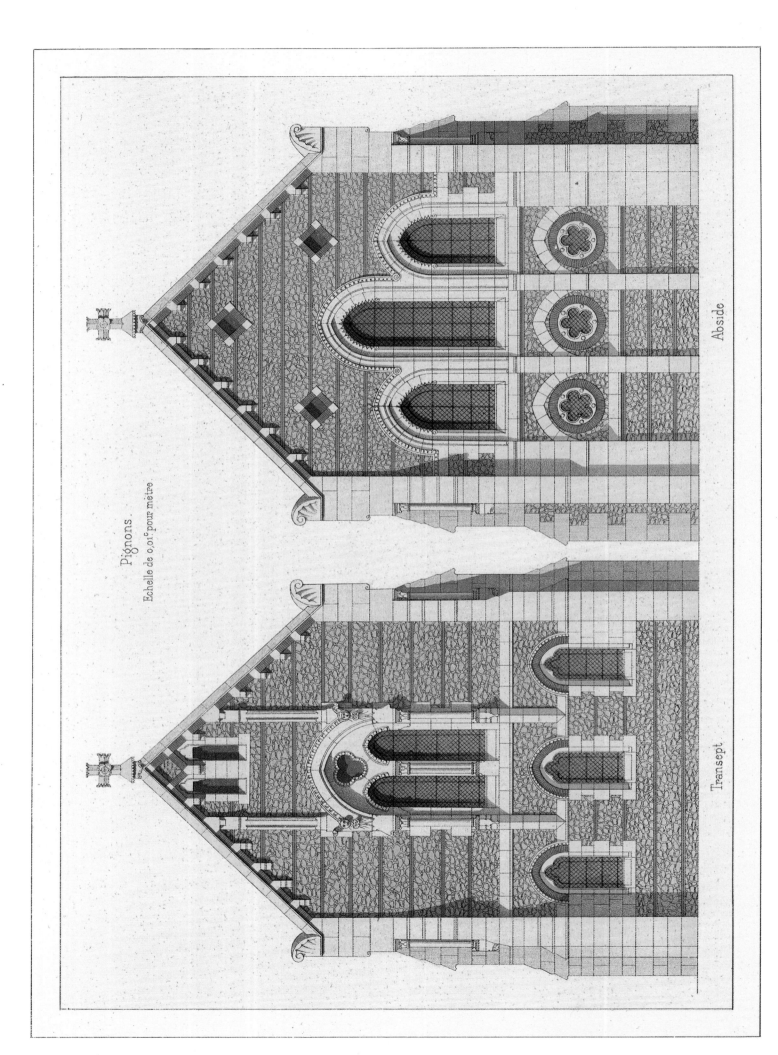

Pignons.

Echelle de 0,01ᵐ pour mètre.

Abside.

Transept.

PLATE 70: Church at Rambouillet (near Versailles); architect: A. de Baudot.

Coupe

Elévation

Echelle de 0,015 p.m.

PLATE 71: House, avenue de l'Observatoire, Paris; architect: Cléry.

PLATE 72: Glazed terra-cotta manufactured by the Müller firm.

PLATE 73: Glazed terra-cotta manufactured by the Müller firm.

Détail du Pavillon d'Angle
Echelle de 0,02 p.m.

PLATE 74: Bishop's palace in Beauvais; architect: E. Vaudremer.

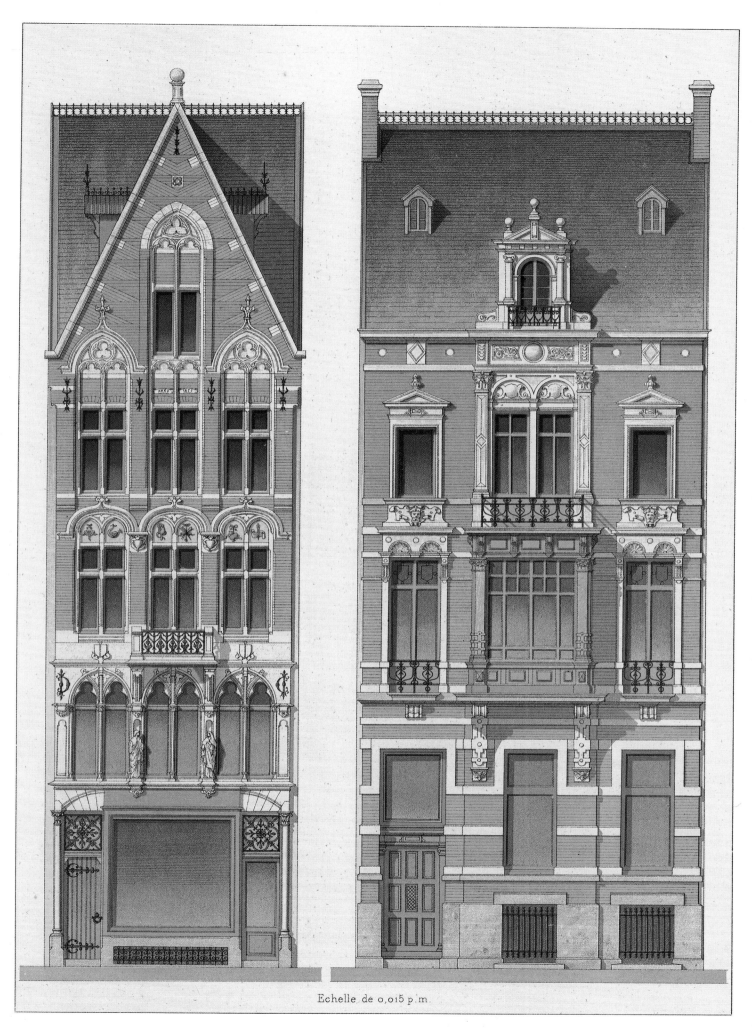

Echelle de 0,015 p. m.

PLATE 75: Houses in Brussels; architect: Mennessier.

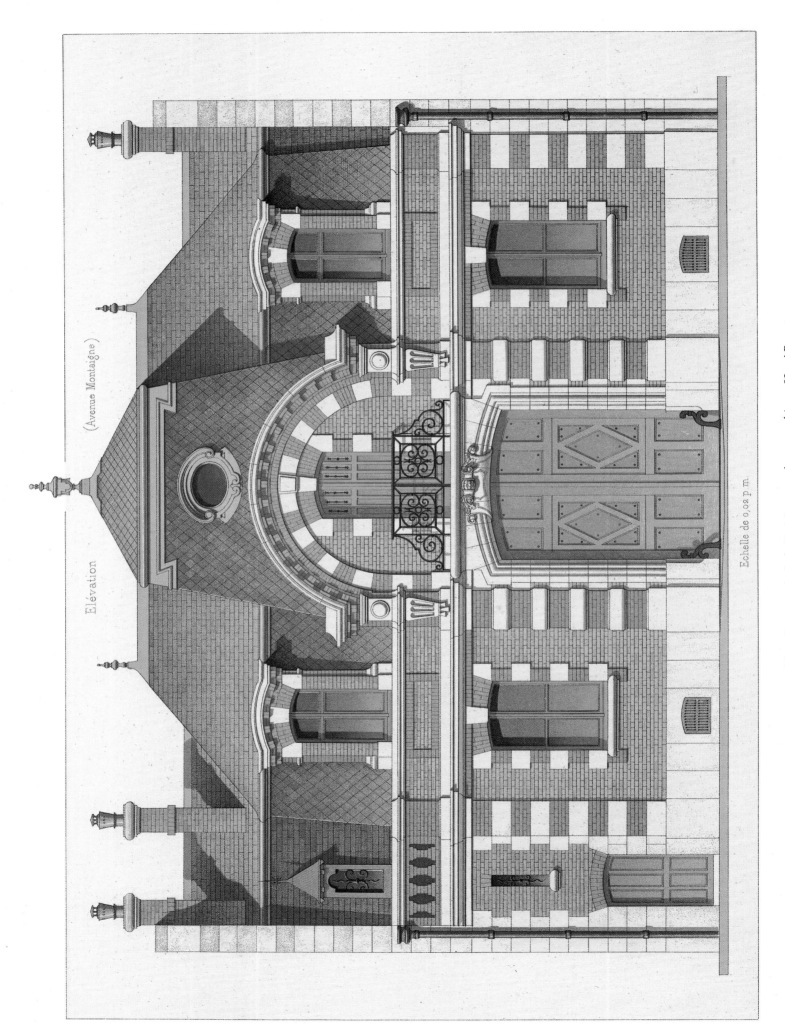

Elévation

(Avenue Montaigne)

Echelle de 0,02 p. m.

PLATE 76: Stable and storage shed of a Parisian town house; architect: Henri Parent.

Elévation (Côté de la rue)
o.^mo15 p. m.

I

II

Echelle de o.^mo4 p. m.

PLATE 77: House in Pontoise (Seine-et-Oise *département*); architect: Pierre Chabat.

PLATE 78: Glazed terra-cotta manufactured by the Loebnitz firm.

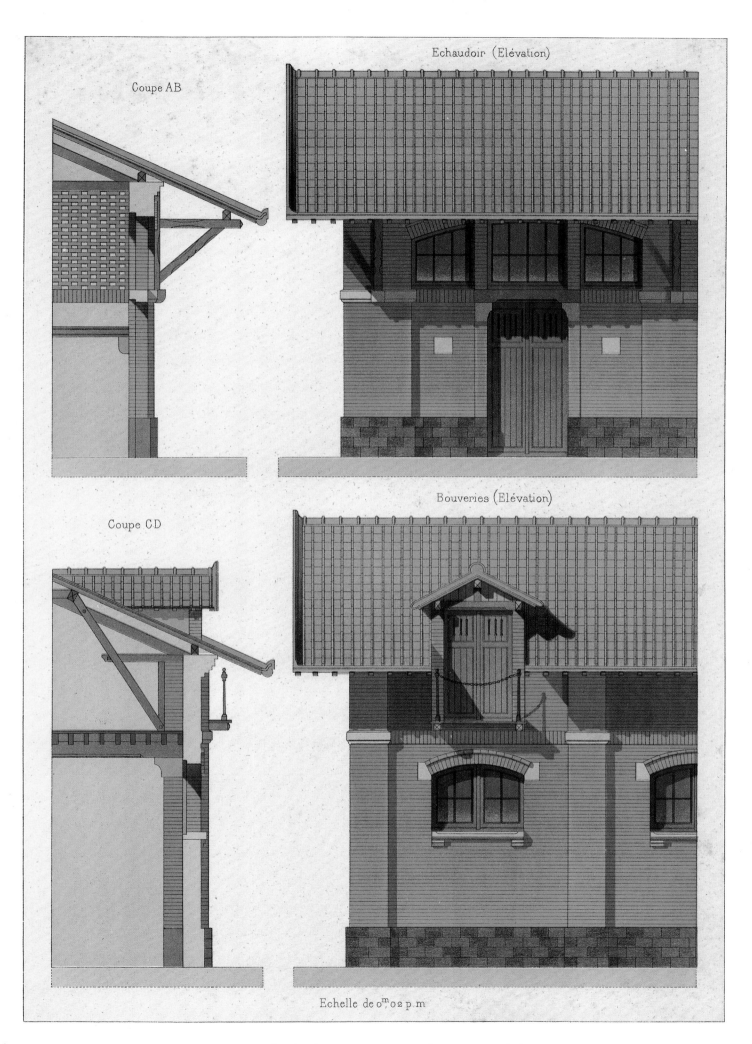

Coupe AB

Echaudoir (Elévation)

Coupe CD

Bouveries (Elévation)

Echelle de 0ᵐ02 p. m

PLATE 79: Slaughterhouse in Pontoise; architect: Pierre Chabat.

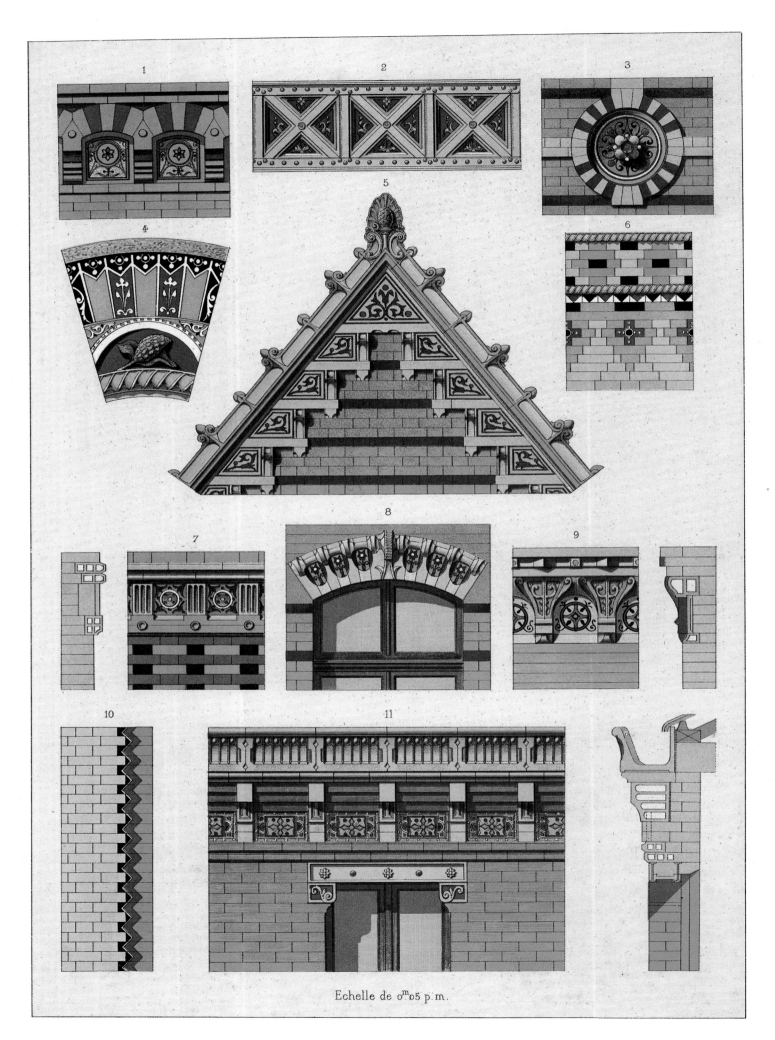

PLATE 80: Decorative details manufactured by the Müller firm.

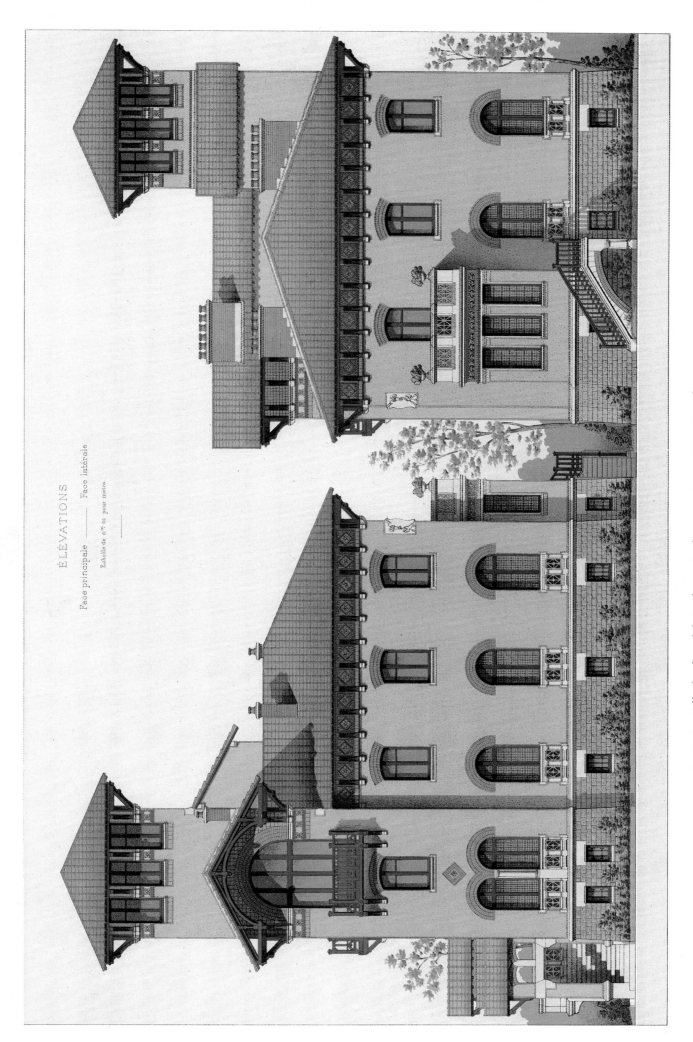

ÉLÉVATIONS

Face principale ———— Face latérale.

Echelle de 0^m 01 pour mètre.

PLATE 81: Villa, boulevard de Boulogne, Boulogne-sur-Seine, 1882–84; architect: Lucien Magne.

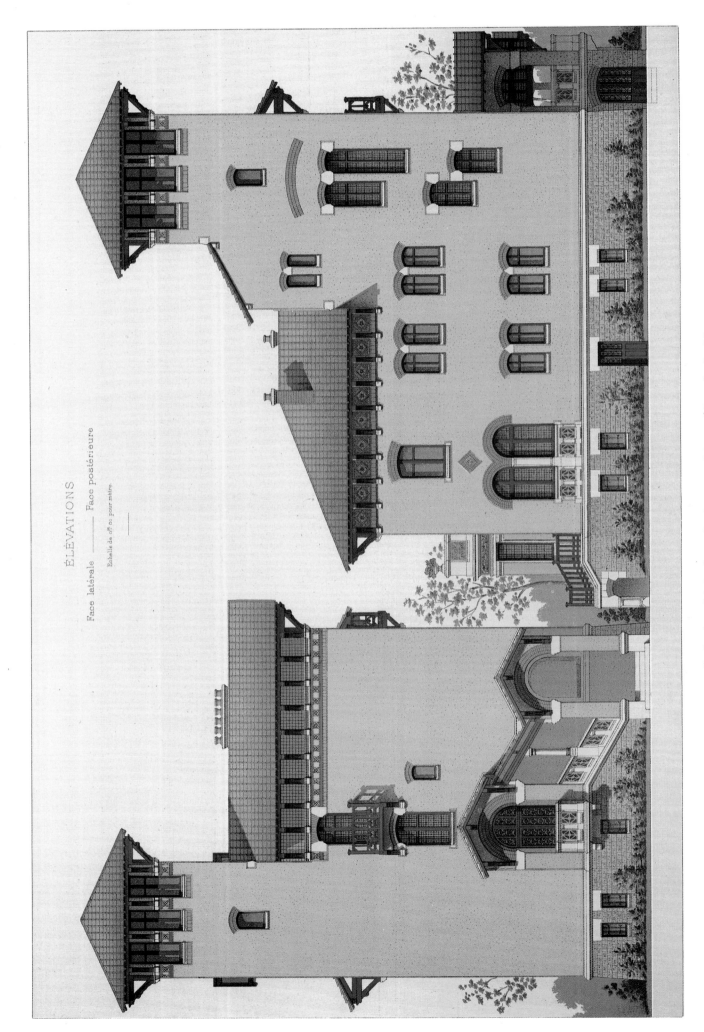

ÉLÉVATIONS

Face latérale ————— Face postérieure

Echelle de 0ᵐ 01 pour mètre.

PLATE 82: Villa, boulevard de Boulogne, Boulogne-sur-Seine; architect: Lucien Magne.

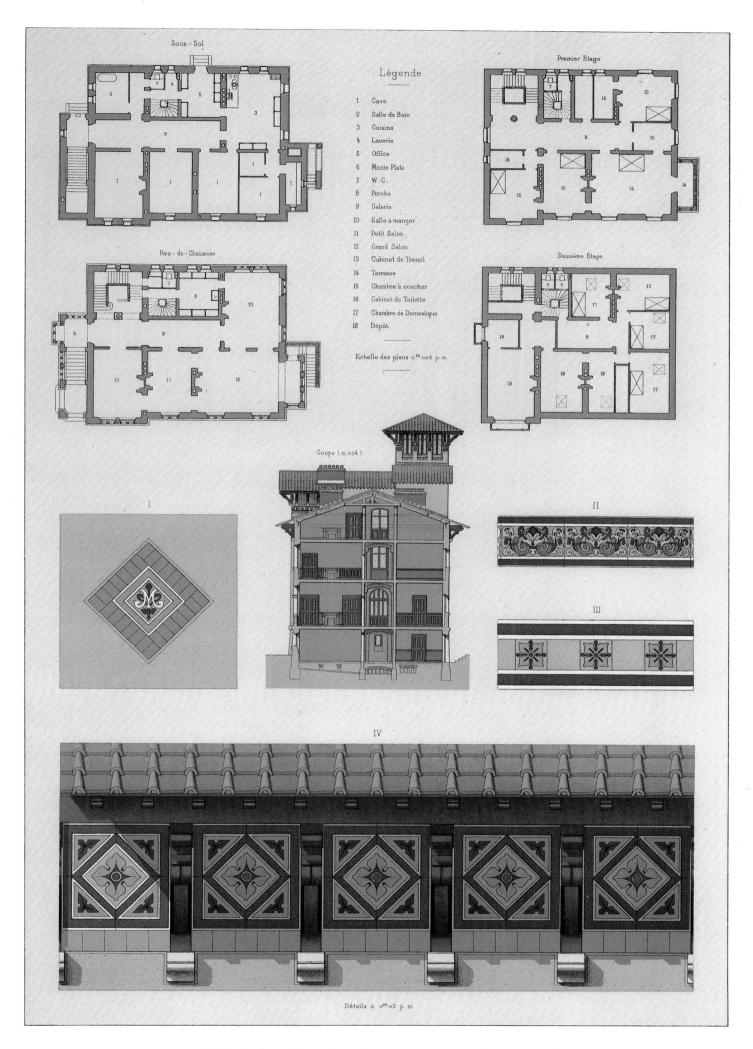

PLATE 83: Villa, boulevard de Boulogne, Boulogne-sur-Seine; architect: Lucien Magne.

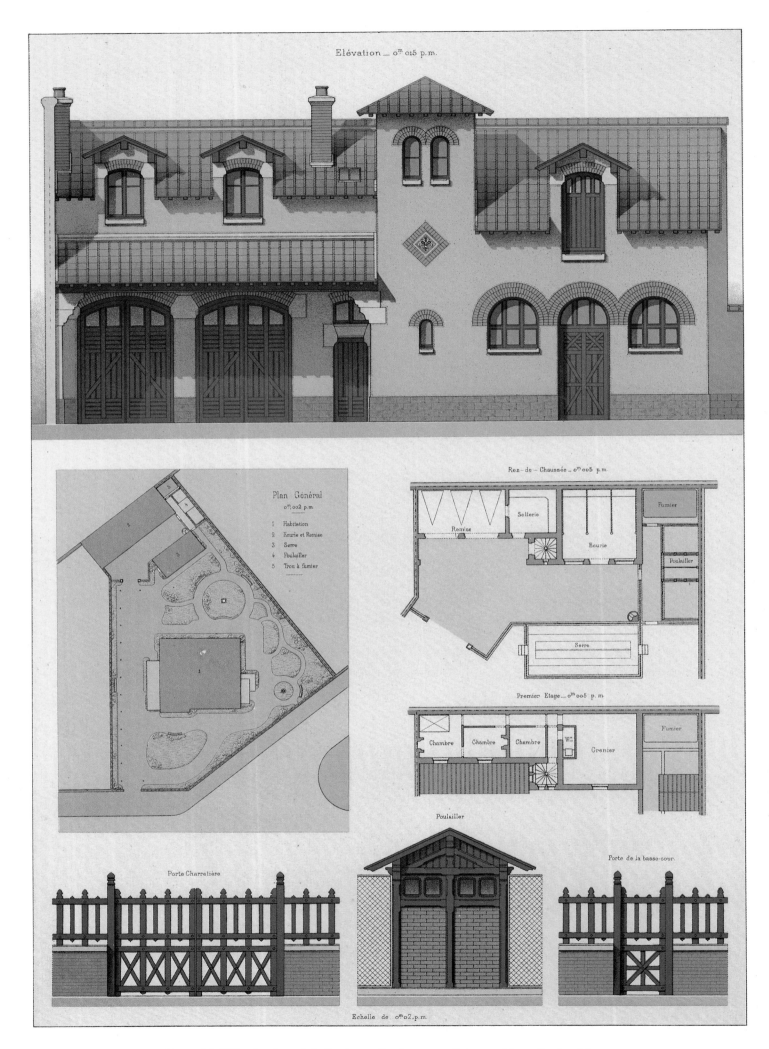

Elévation — 0ᵐ 015 p.m.

Plan Général
0ᵐ, 002 p.m
1 Habitation
2 Ecurie et Remise
3 Serre
4 Poulailler
5 Trou à fumier

Rez-de-Chaussée — 0ᵐ 005 p.m.

Remise   Sellerie   Fumier
Ecurie   Poulailler
Serre

Premier Etage — 0ᵐ 005 p.m.

Chambre Chambre Chambre W.C. Grenier   Fumier

Poulailler

Porte Charretière   Porte de la basse-cour.

Echelle de 0ᵐ 02.p.m.

PLATE 84: Villa, boulevard de Boulogne, Boulogne-sur-Seine; architect: Lucien Magne.

Elévation.

Plan

(0ᵐ o25 p.m.)

Face latérale.

Coupe.

Légende

1. Poulailler.
2. Pigeonnier.
3. Lapinières.

Elévations et Coupe _ 0ᵐ o3 p.m.

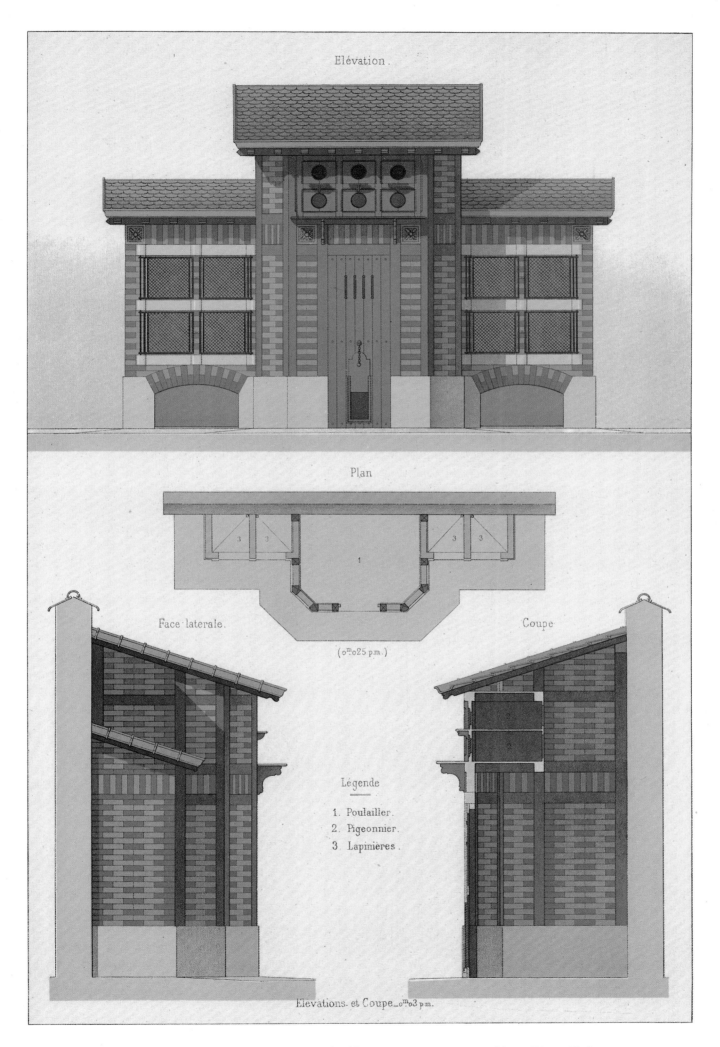

PLATE 85: House for chickens, pigeons and rabbits at Bagneux (Paris); architect: Pierre Chabat.

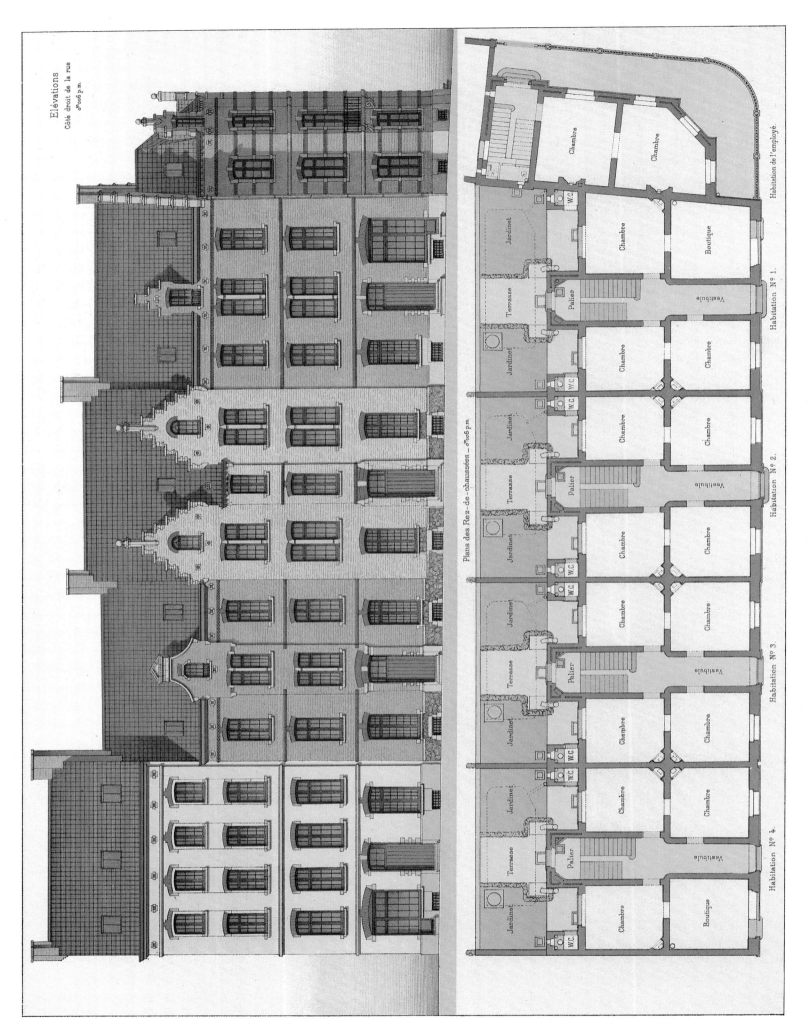

PLATE 86: Residential units for Brussels gas workers, Laeken; architect: V. Jamaer.

PLATE 87: Villa at Luzarches (north of Paris); architect: Tronquois.

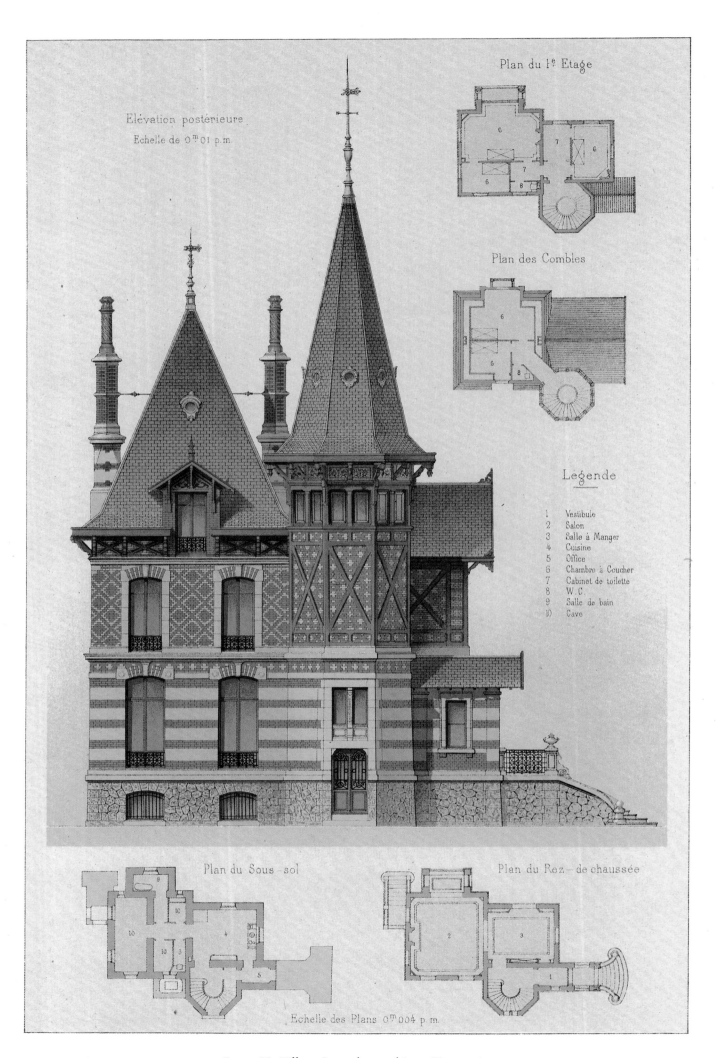

Plan du 1º. Etage

Elévation postérieure
Echelle de 0ᵐ.01 p.m.

Plan des Combles

Legende

1   Vestibule
2   Salon
3   Salle à Manger
4   Cuisine
5   Office
6   Chambre à Coucher
7   Cabinet de toilette
8   W.C.
9   Salle de bain
10   Cave

Plan du Sous-sol

Plan du Rez—de chaussée

Echelle des Plans 0ᵐ.004 p.m.

PLATE 88: Villa at Luzarches; architect: Tronquois.

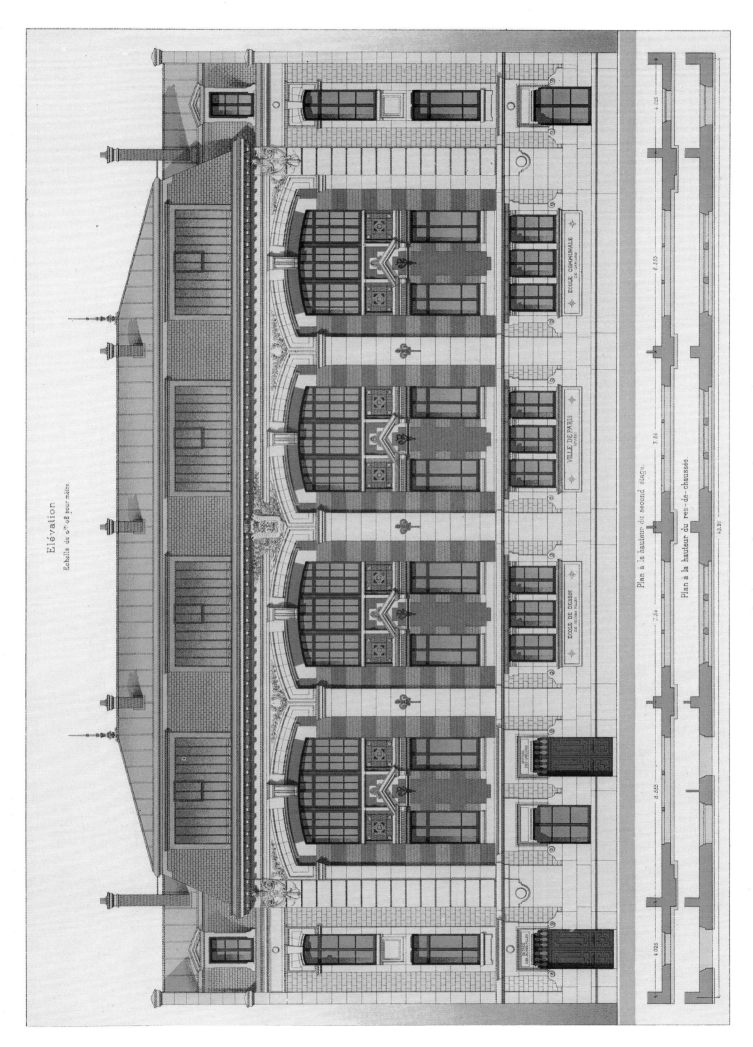

PLATE 89: School, rue Madame, Paris; architect: H. Erard.

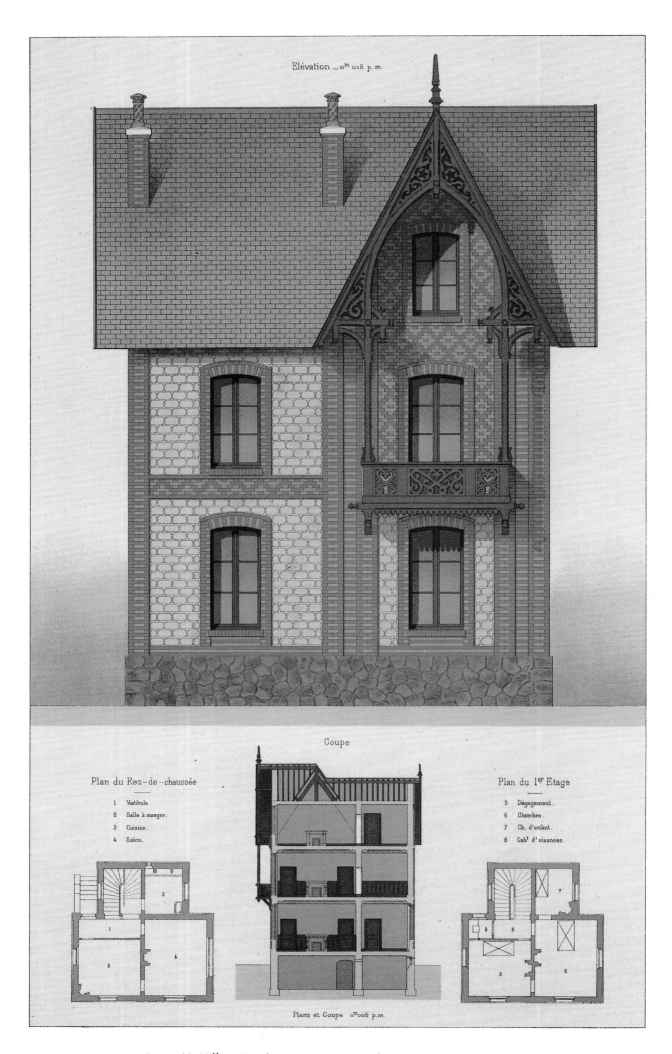

Elévation _ 0^m015 p. m.

Coupe

Plan du Rez-de-chaussée

1   Vestibule.
2   Salle à manger.
3   Cuisine.
4   Salon.

Plan du 1er Etage

5   Dégagement.
6   Chambre.
7   Ch. d'enfant.
8   Cab^t d'aisances.

Plans et Coupe   0^m005 p. m.

PLATE 90: Villa at Le Vésinet (Seine-et-Oise *département*); architect: Héret.

PLATE 91: Chalet d'Ambricourt at Villers-sur-Mer (Calvados *département*); architect: A. Feine.

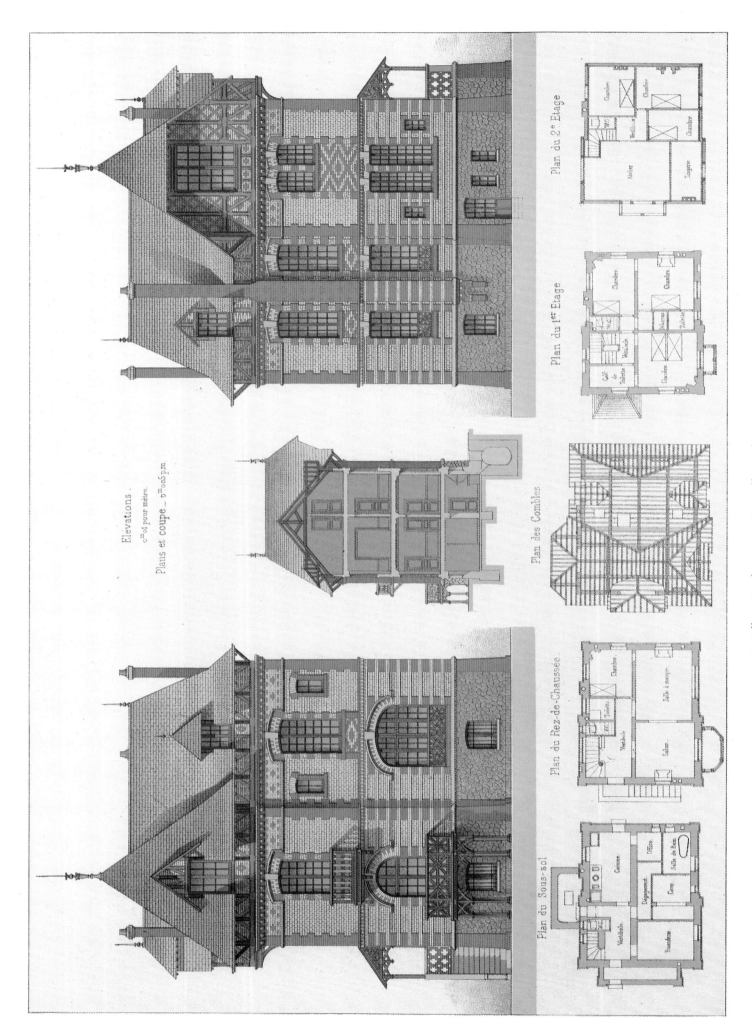

Élevations.
o^mo1 pour mètre.
Plans et coupe_ o^moo5p.m

Plan des Combles

Plan du 2e Etage

Plan du 1er Etage

Plan du Rez-de-Chaussée.

Plan du Sous-sol

PLATE 92: Villa at Houlgate (near Deauville); architect: E. Papinot.

PLATE 93: Engine shed, Lamothe station (Southern line).

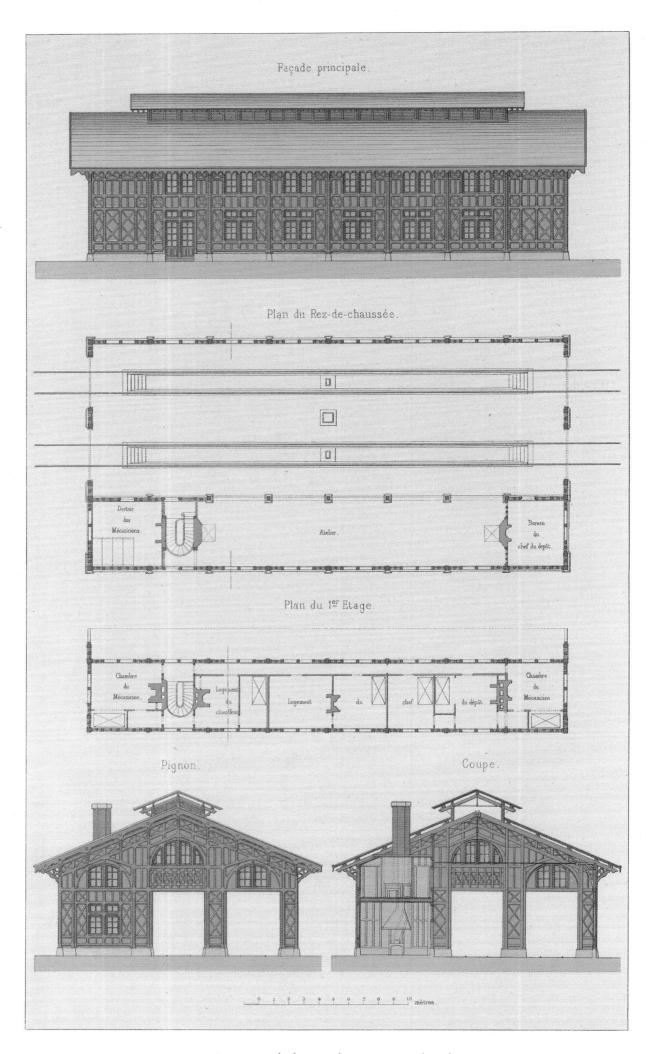

Façade principale.

Plan du Rez-de-chaussée.

Dortoir des Mécaniciens.

Atelier.

Bureau du chef du dépôt.

Plan du 1er Etage.

Chambre du Mécanicien.

Logement du chauffeur

Logement du chef du dépôt.

Chambre du Mécanicien.

Pignon.

Coupe.

0 1 2 3 4 5 6 7 8 9 10 mètres.

PLATE 94: Engine shed, Lamothe station (Southern line).

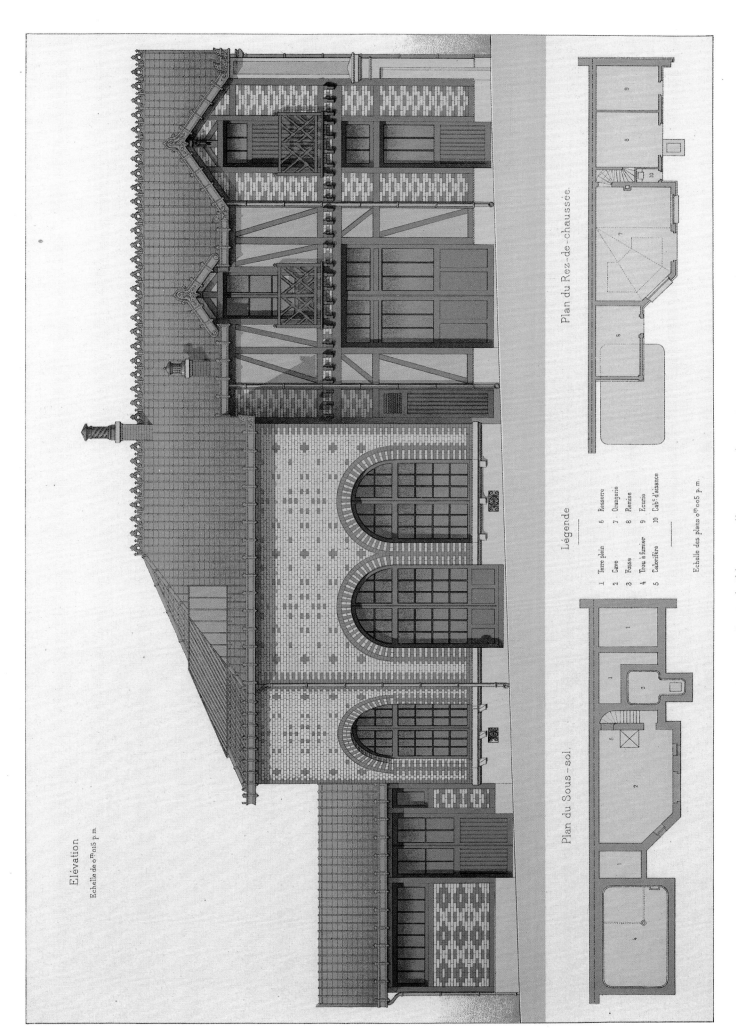

Elévation

Echelle de o.^mo15 p. m.

Plan du Rez-de-chaussée.

Plan du Sous-sol.

Légende

1 Terre plein	6 Ressorre
2 Cave	7 Orangerie
3 Fosse	8 Remise
4 Trou à fumier	9 Ecurie
5 Calorifère	10 Cab.^t d'aisance

Echelle des plans o.^moo5 p. m.

PLATE 95: Service building, Neuilly (Paris); architect: Simonet.

Détail o^mo4 p.m.   Plan o^moo4 p.m.   Détail o^mo4 p.m.

Classe

Classe

PLATE 96: Nursery school in Dunkerque (Dunkirk); architects: Lecoq and Delanoye.

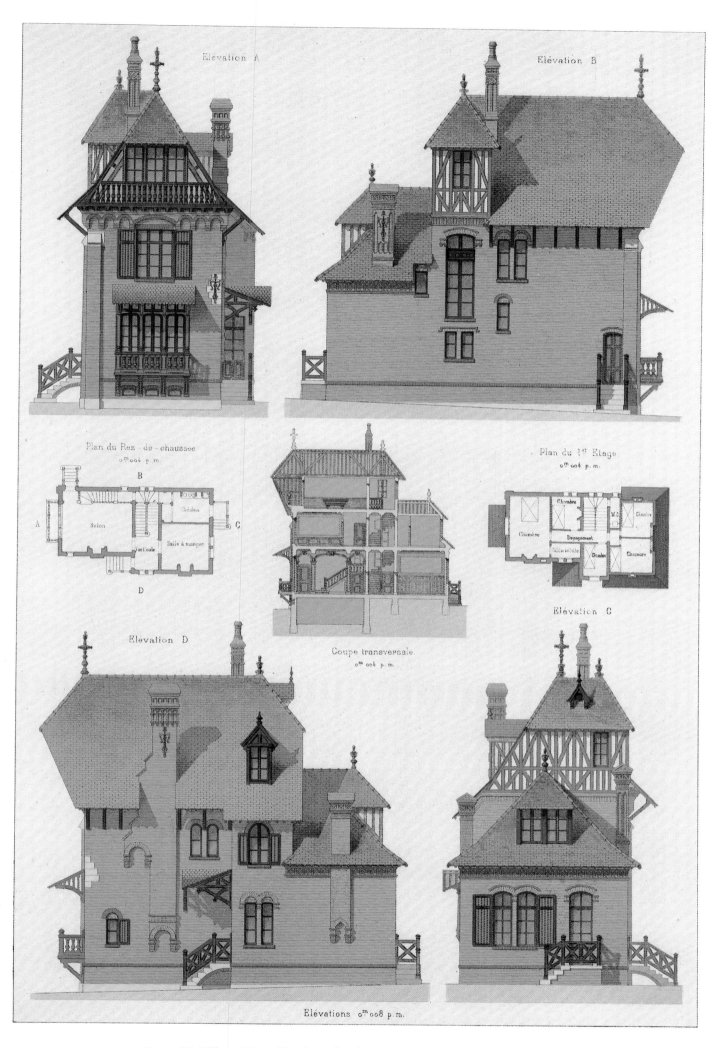

Elévation A

Elévation B

Plan du Rez - de - chaussée
0ᵐ004 p. m.

B

A   Salon   Cuisine   C
        Vestibule   Salle à manger

D

Coupe transversale.
0ᵐ004 p. m.

Plan du 1ᵉʳ Etage
0ᵐ004 p. m.

Chambre
Chambre   Chambre
        Dégagement
Cabinet toilette   Chambre   Chambre

Elévation C

Elévation D

Elévations 0ᵐ008 p. m.

PLATE 97: Villa at Bénerville (Calvados *département*); architect: A. Mussigmann.

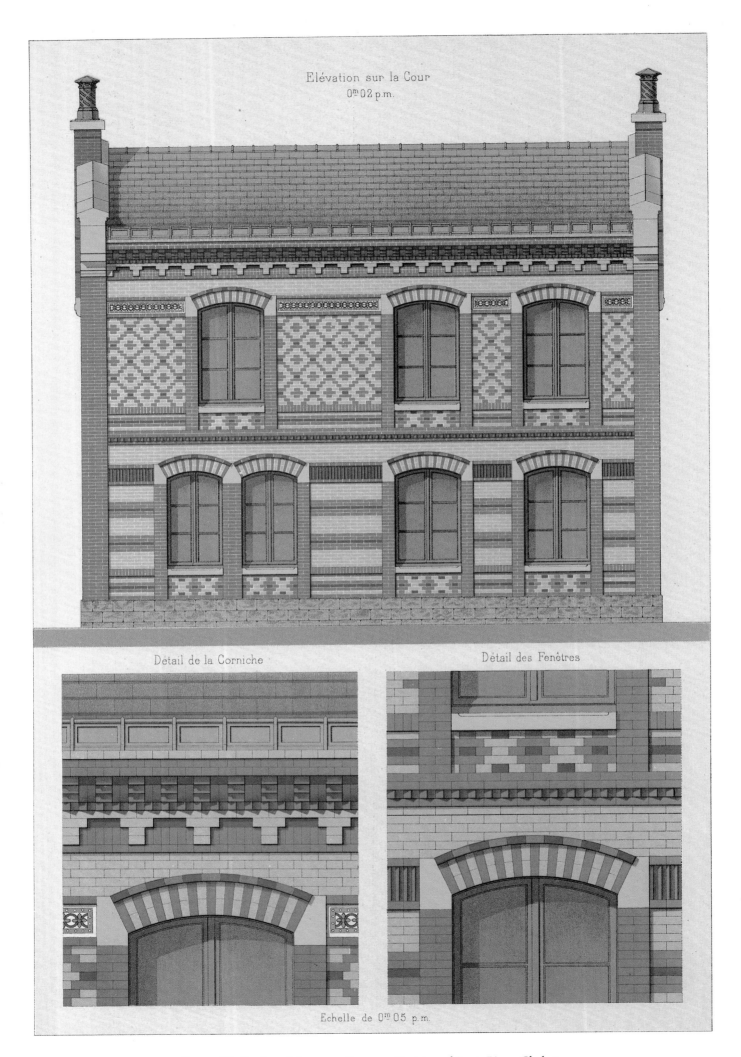

Elévation sur la Cour
0^m02 p.m.

Détail de la Corniche

Détail des Fenêtres

Echelle de 0^m05 p.m.

PLATE 98: Gardener's house at Bagneux (Paris); architect: Pierre Chabat.

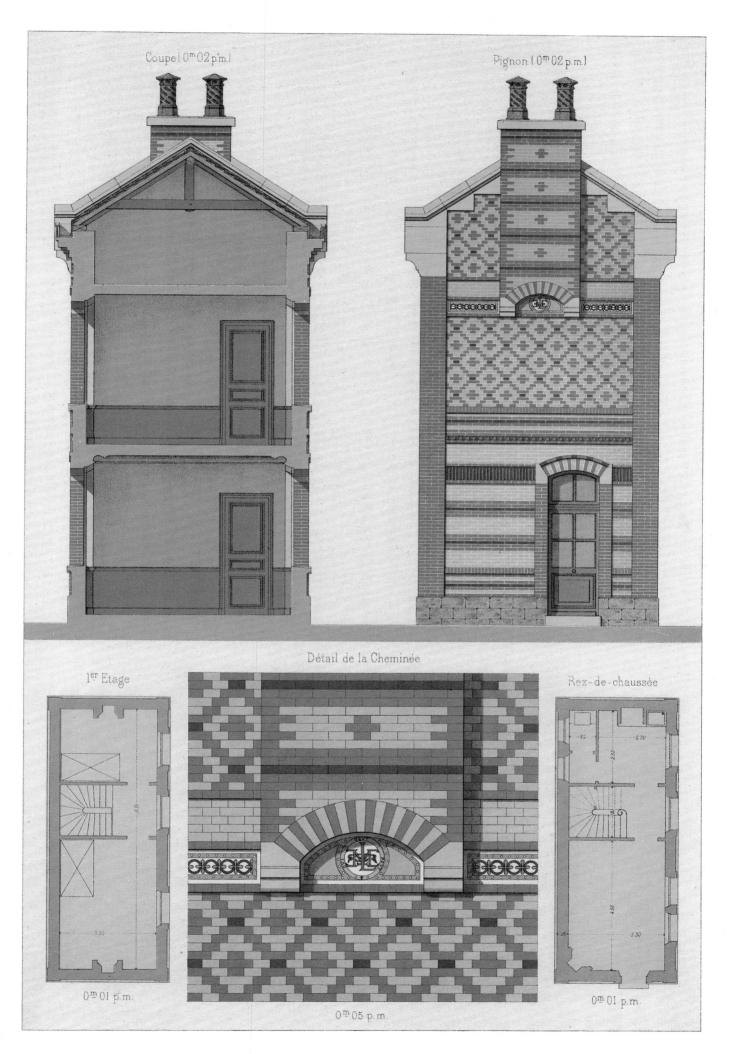

Coupe (0ᵐ 02 p.m.)

Pignon (0ᵐ 02 p.m.)

Détail de la Cheminée

1ᵉʳ Etage

Rez-de-chaussée

0ᵐ 01 p.m.

0ᵐ 05 p.m.

0ᵐ 01 p.m.

PLATE 99: Gardener's house at Bagneux (Paris); architect: Pierre Chabat.

Elévation sur la rue

Echelle de o^mo25 pour mètre.

PLATE 100: Villa "Mon Caprice," Villers-sur-Mer (Calvados *département*); architect: Eugène Macé; decorator: A. Darvant.

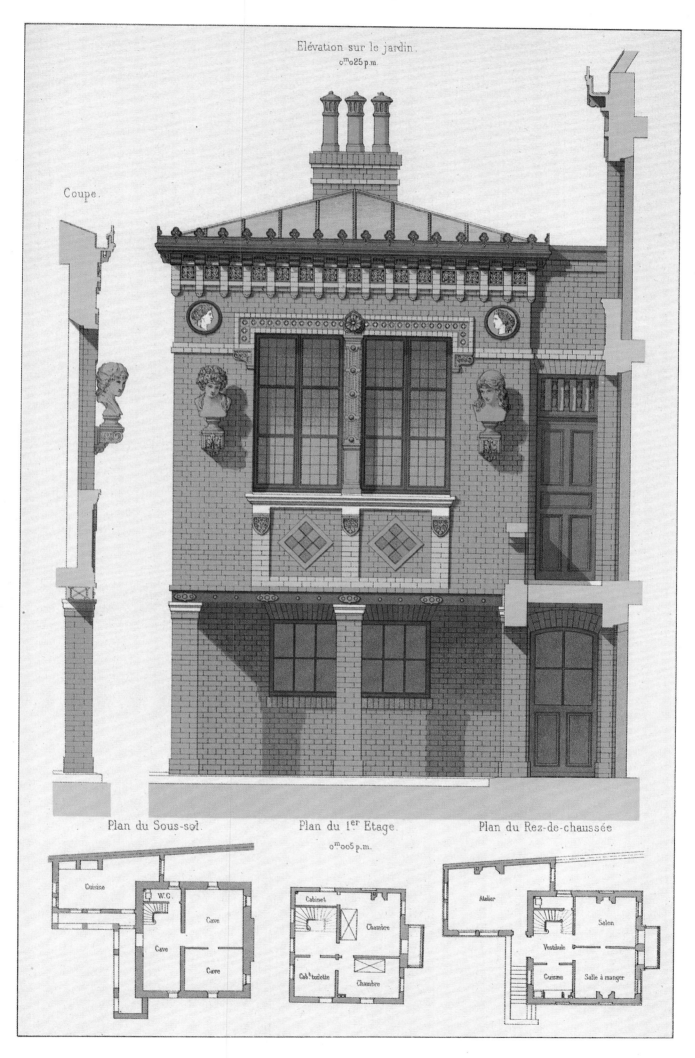

Elévation sur le jardin.
0^mo25 p.m.

Coupe.

Plan du Sous-sol.   Plan du 1er Etage.   Plan du Rez-de-chaussée
0^moo5 p.m.

Cuisine   W.C.   Cabinet   Atelier
Cave   Chambre   Salon
Cave   Cab.^t toilette   Vestibule
Cave   Chambre   Cuisine   Salle à manger

PLATE 101: Villa "Mon Caprice," Villers-sur-Mer; architect: Eugène Macé; decorator: A. Darvant.

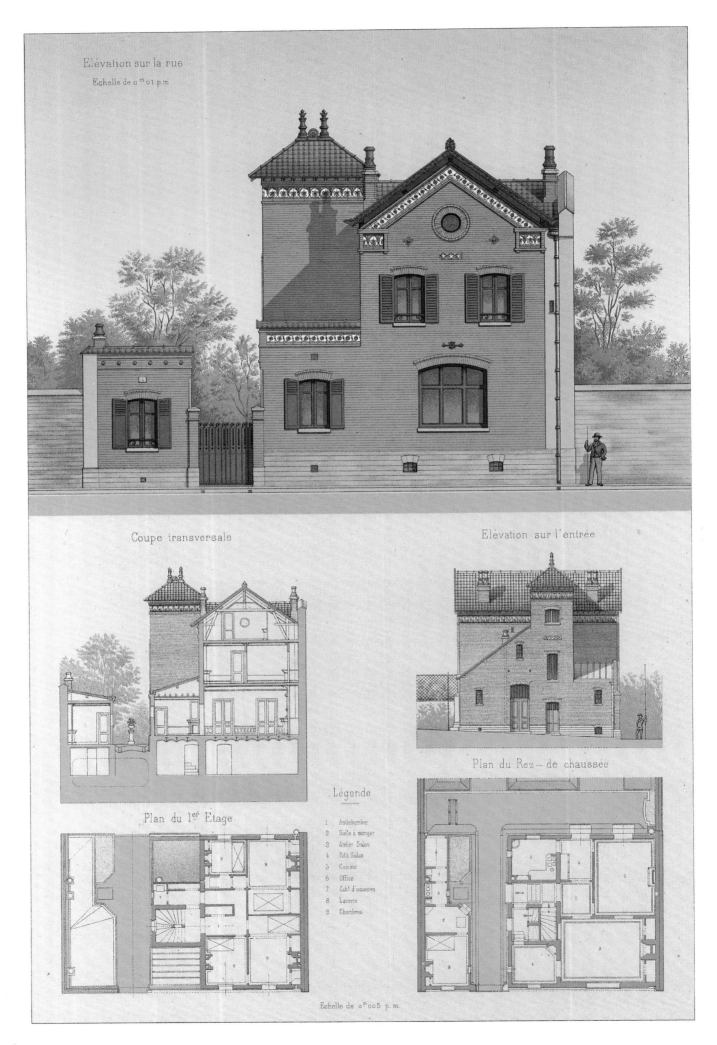

Elévation sur la rue

Echelle de 0m01 p.m.

Coupe transversale

Elévation sur l'entrée

Plan du Rez—de chaussée

Légende

1   Antichambre
2   Salle à manger
3   Atelier Salon
4   Petit Salon
5   Cuisine
6   Office
7   Cab.t d'aisances
8   Laverie
9   Chambres

Plan du 1er Etage

Echelle de 0m005 p.m.

PLATE 102: House, rue Friant, Paris; architect: A. Hédin.

Pignon (0,005 p.m.)

Plan (0ᵐ0025 p.m.)

Coupe (0,005 p.m.)

Élevation (0,01 p.m.)

A

B

PLATE 103: Market.

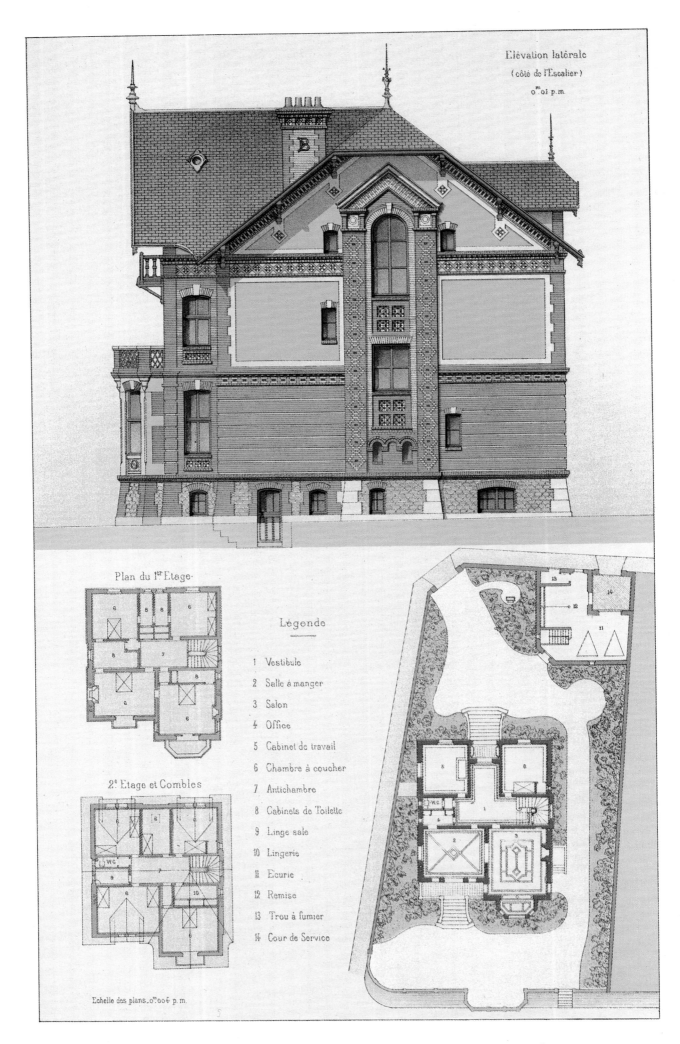

Élévation latérale
(côté de l'Escalier)
0ᵐ.01 p.m.

Plan du 1ᵉʳ Étage.

2ᵉ. Étage et Combles

Échelle des plans. 0ᵐ.004 p. m.

Légende

1 Vestibule

2 Salle à manger

3 Salon

4 Office

5 Cabinet de travail

6 Chambre à coucher

7 Antichambre

8 Cabinets de Toilette

9 Linge sale

10 Lingerie

11 Écurie

12 Remise

13 Trou à fumier

14 Cour de Service

PLATE 104: Villa "Marguerite" at Houlgate (near Deauville); architect: E.-M. Auburtin.

Elévation (coté de la mer)

0ᵐ o1 p. m.

PLATE 105: Villa "Marguerite" at Houlgate; architect: E.-M. Auburtin.

Coupe longitudinale

0^m 004 p. m.

Elévation (coté de l'entrée)

0^m 01 p. m.

PLATE 106: Villa "Marguerite" at Houlgate; architect: E.-M. Auburtin.

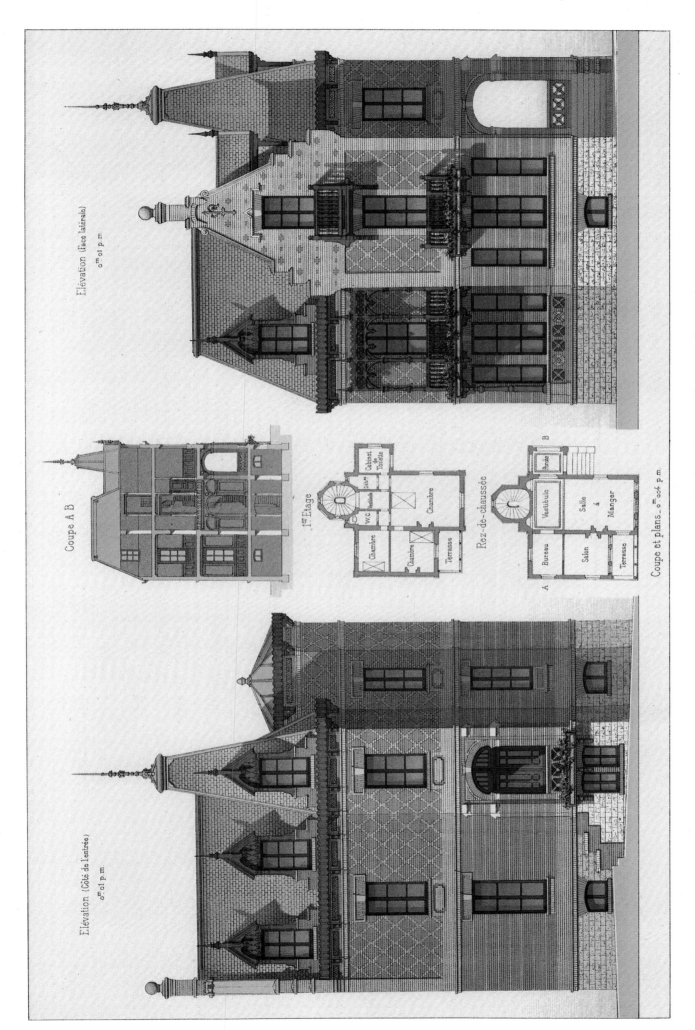

Élévation (face latérale)
0.m.01 p.m

Coupe A B

1er Étage

Chambre
Chambre
Terrasse
W.C
Débar
Vestibule
Cabinet de Toilette
Chambre

Rez-de-chaussée

A
Bureau
Salon
Terrasse
Vestibule
Salle à Manger
Perron
B

Coupe et plans _0.m 004 p. m.

Élévation (Côté de l'entrée)
0.m.01 p.m.

PLATE 107: Villa "Adélia" at Villers-sur-Mer (Calvados *département*); architect: Eugène Macé.

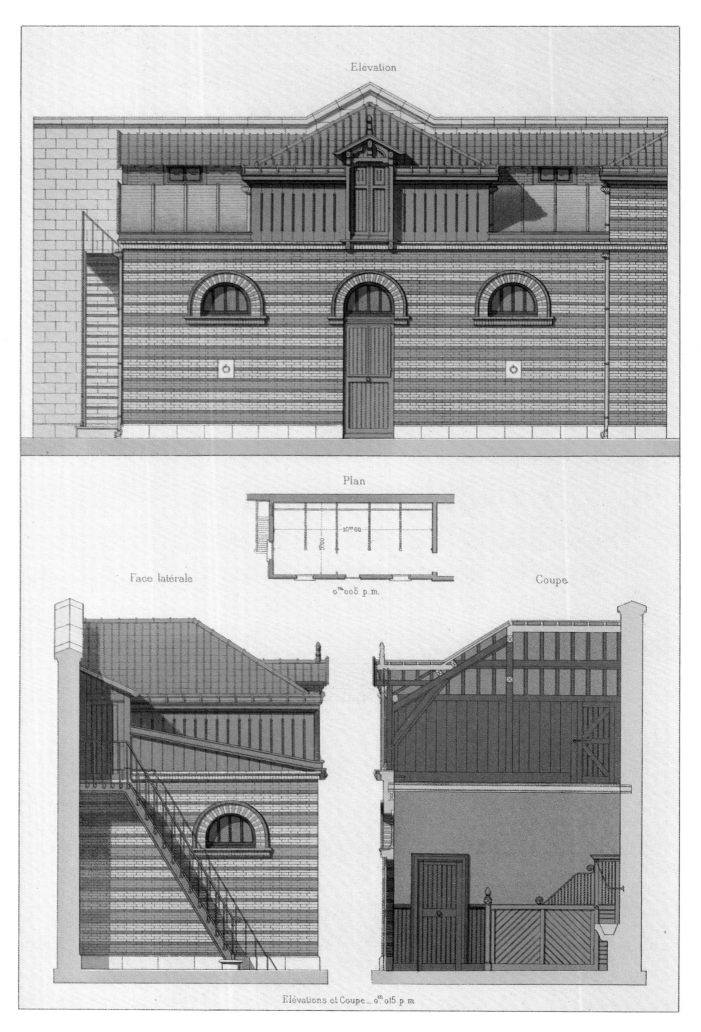

Élévation

Plan

10ᵐ 60

0ᵐ oo5 p.m.

Face latérale

Coupe

Élévations et Coupe _ 0ᵐ o15 p. m.

PLATE 108: Stables of a town house on boulevard Beauséjour, Paris; architect; Pierre Chabat.

Coupe perspective sur les terrasses.

(Côté de la Seine)

PLATE 109: Restaurant de Bercy (Paris); architect: Lheureux.

Elévation principale
0^mo15 p.m.

Coupe Longitudinale
0^moo5 p.m.

Rez-de-Chaussée
0^moo5 p.m.

Cuisine

Salle
à
manger

Cab.^t
du
Travail

Salon

1er Etage.
0^moo5 p.m.

Chambre

Chambre

Chambre

Chambre

PLATE 110: House at Veules (near Dieppe); architect: Paul Déchard.

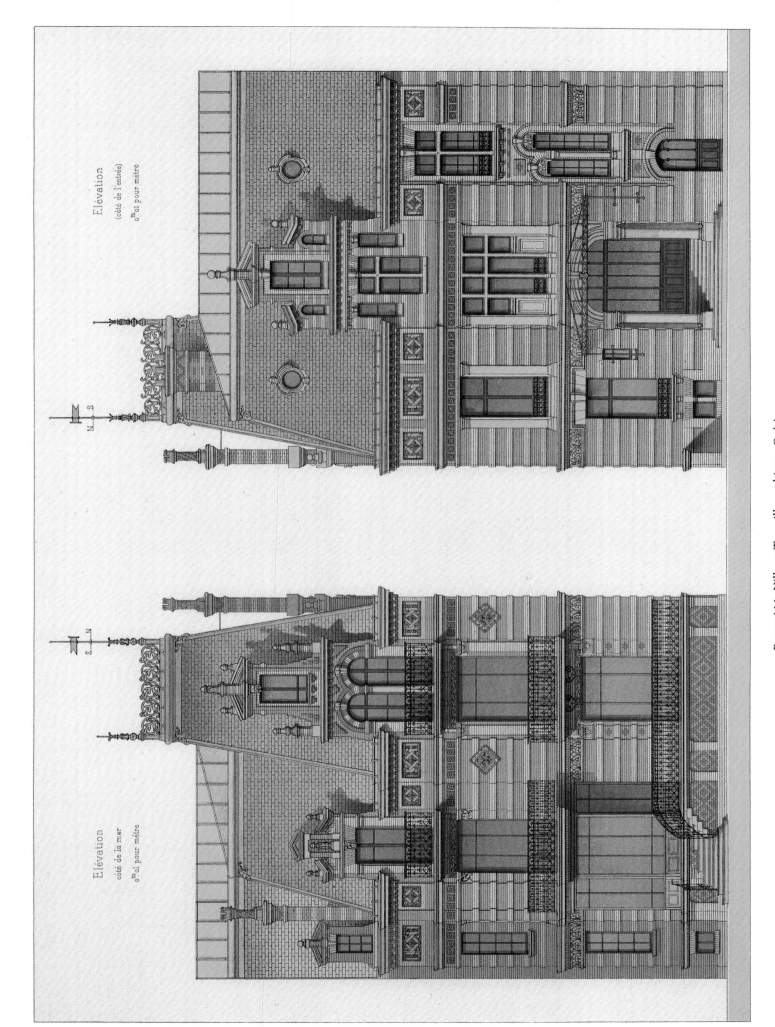

Elévation
(côté de l'entrée)
0.^m.01 pour mètre

Elévation
côté de la mer
0.^m.01 pour mètre

PLATE 111: Villa at Trouville; architect: Guérinot.

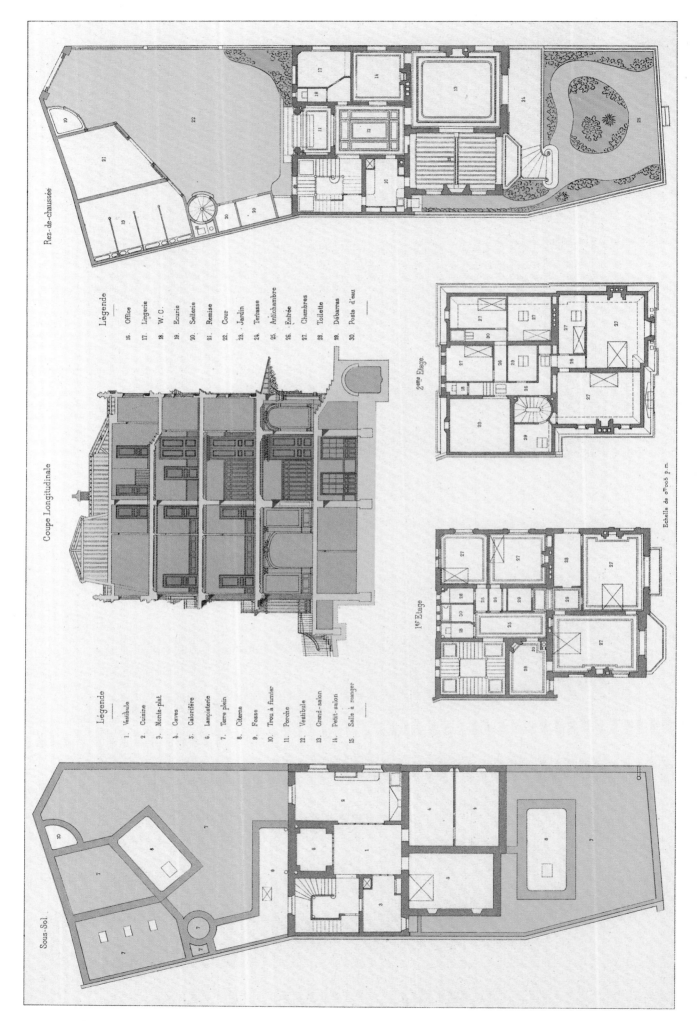

Rez-de-chaussée

Coupe Longitudinale

Sous-Sol.

Légende

16. Office
17. Lingerie
18. W. C.
19. Écurie
20. Sellerie
21. Remise
22. Cour
23. Jardin
24. Terrasse
25. Antichambre
26. Entrée
27. Chambres
28. Toilette
29. Débarras
30. Poste d'eau

Légende

1. Vestibule
2. Cuisine
3. Monte-plat
4. Caves
5. Calorifère
6. Lampisterie
7. Terre plein
8. Citerne
9. Fosse
10. Trou à fumier
11. Porche
12. Vestibule
13. Grand-salon
14. Petit-salon
15. Salle à manger

2ème Étage.

1er Étage

Échelle de 0m005 p.m.

PLATE 112: Villa at Trouville; architect: Guérinot.

PLATE 113: The Eugène Decan villa at Villers-sur-Mer (Calvados *département*).

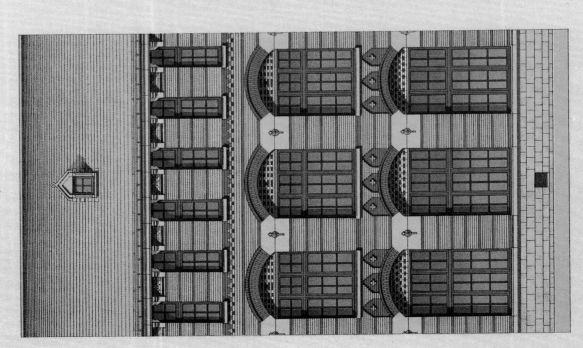

Elévation

Rez-de-chaussée: Classes et études
1er_2ème Etage: Dortoirs.

Elévation

Rez-de-chaussée: Réfectoire_1er Etage: Classes et études
2ème Etage: Dortoirs.

Elévation

Rez-de-chaussée et 1er Etage: Classes et études
2ème Etage: Dortoirs.

Echelle de 0m01 pour mètre

PLATE 114: The Lycée (boarding high school) Lakanal at Sceaux (Paris); architect: A. de Baudot.

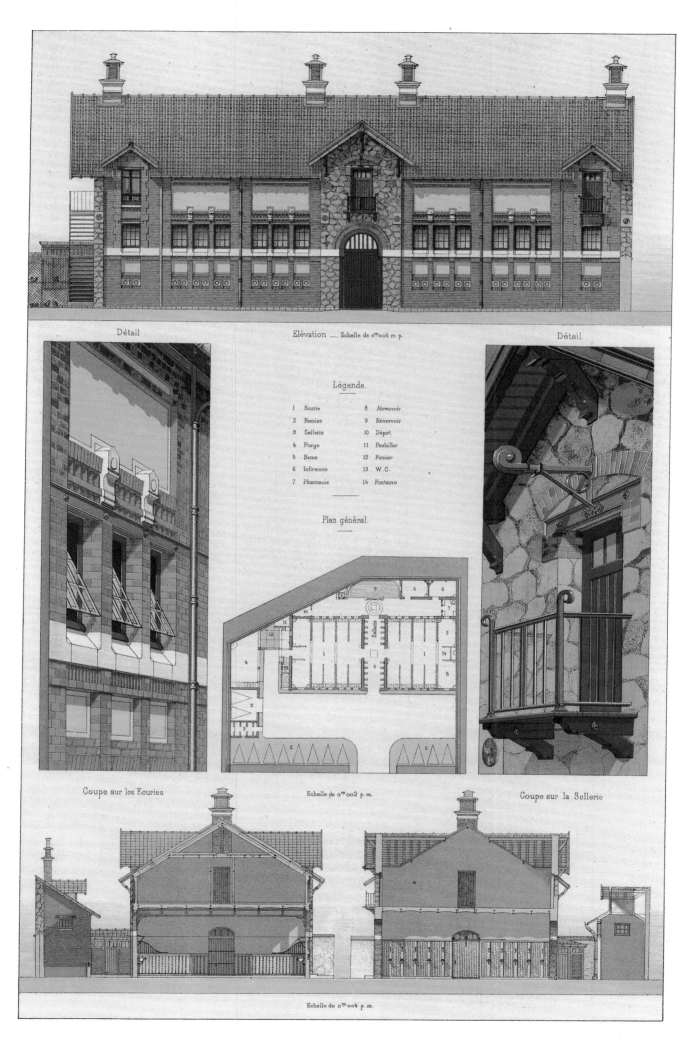

Détail

Elévation — Echelle de 0ᵐ006 m.p.

Détail

Légende.

1	Ecurie	8	Abreuvoir
2	Remise	9	Réservoir
3	Sellerie	10	Dépot
4	Forge	11	Poulailler
5	Boxe	12	Fumier
6	Infirmerie	13	W.C.
7	Pharmacie	14	Fontaine

Plan général.

Coupe sur les Ecuries

Echelle de 0ᵐ002 p.m.

Coupe sur la Sellerie

Echelle de 0ᵐ004 p.m.

PLATE 115: Merchant's stables, rue Cros, Paris; architect: L. Lethorel.

Elévation _o^m o2 p.m.

Coupe

Plan du Rez-de-chaussée

W.C.
Sellerie
Ecurie
Remise

Plan du 1er Etage

Cour
Dégagement
Chambre
Chambre
Chambre

I

II

o^m o4 p.m.

Echelle de o^m oo5 p.m.

o^m o4 p.m.

PLATE 116: Service buildings of a town house, rue Vernet, Paris; architect: Paul Sédille.

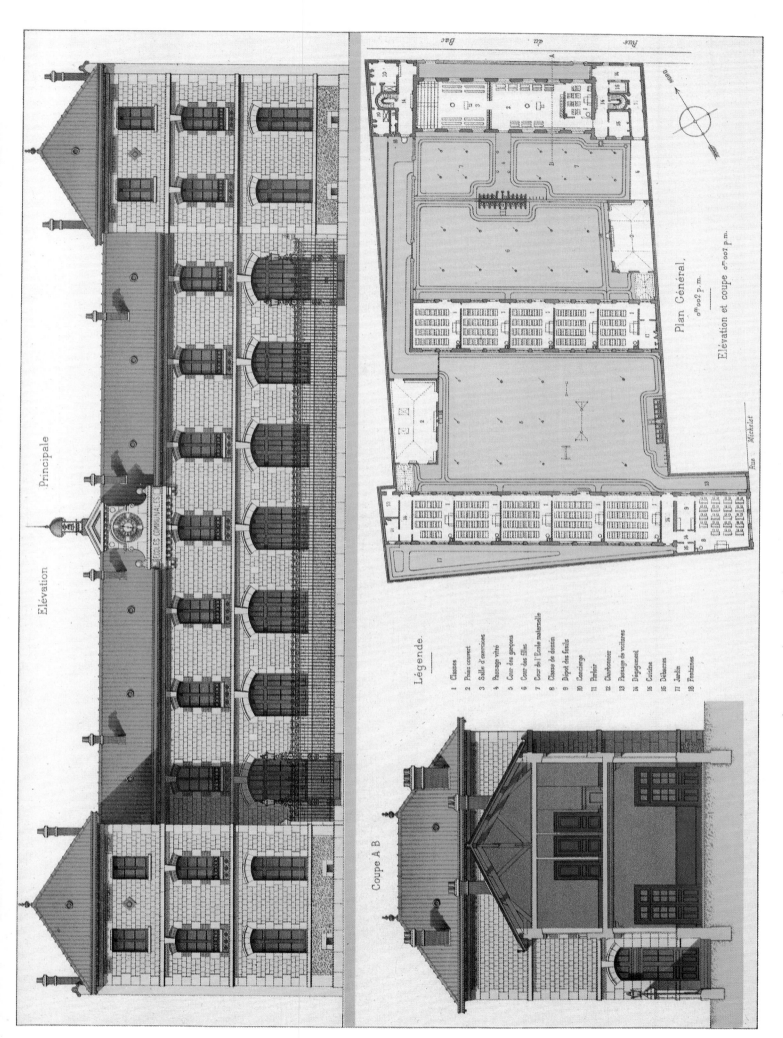

PLATE 117: Elementary and nursery school at Saint-Maur-les-Fossés (near Paris); architect: F. Marin.

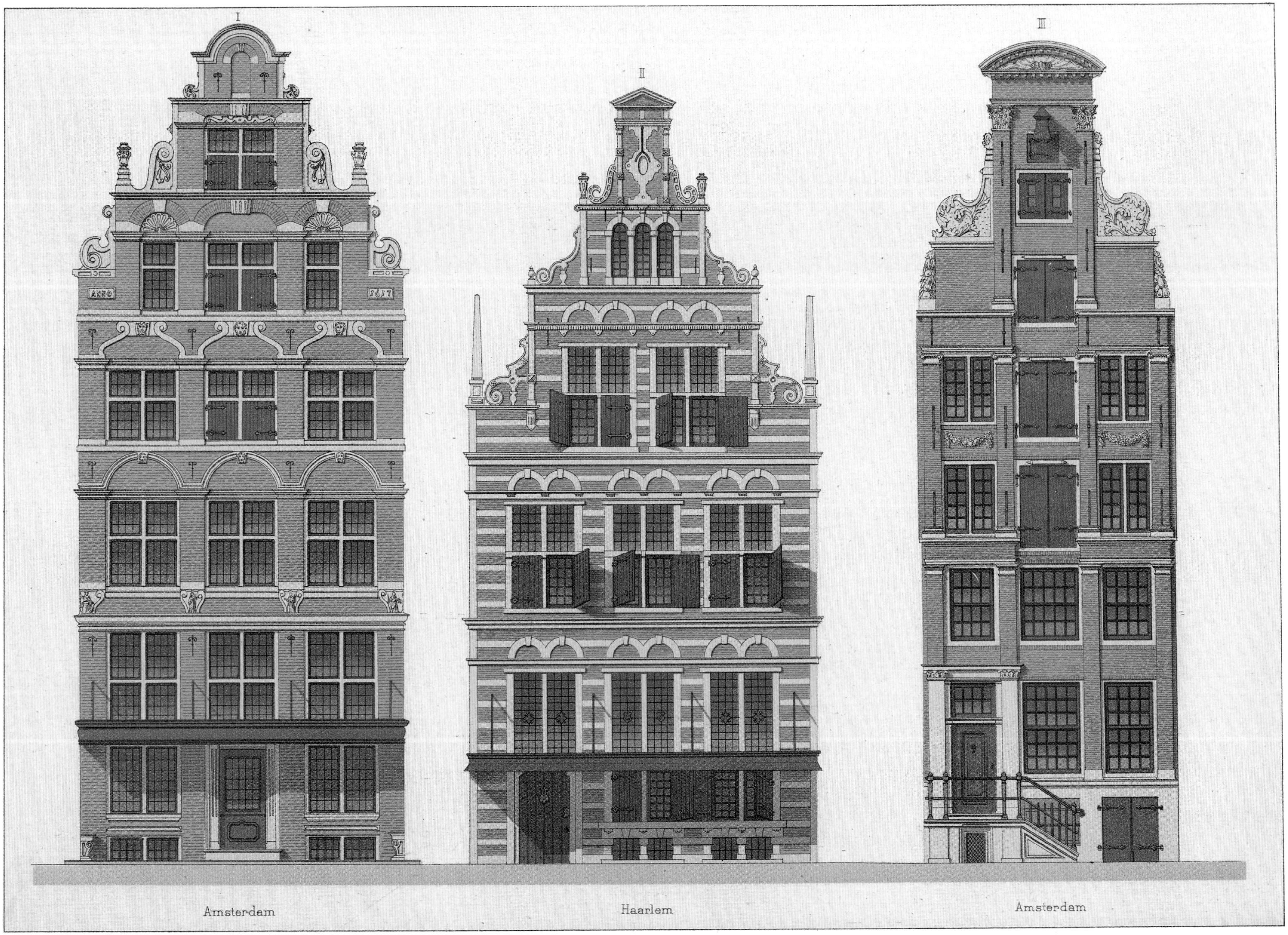

I   Amsterdam   II   Haarlem   III   Amsterdam

PLATE 118: Dutch houses of the 16th and 17th centuries.

Elévation principale

0ᵐ.015 pour métre

PLATE 119: Villa Brodu at Beuzéval (Calvados *département*); architect: Baumier.

Elévation

(Côté de l'entrée principale)

0ᵐ.012 p.m

Sous-sol

Cave

Caveau

Dépôt | Vestibule | Dépôt

Cuisine

Salle des Gens

W.C

Buverie | Charbon

Rez-de-chaussée

Cabinet de travail

W.C

Vestiaire

Office

Vestibule

Salle à Manger

Salon

1ᵉʳ Etage

Chambre

W.C

Lingerie

Cabᵗ de Toilette

Chambre

Chambre

Echelle des plans 0ᵐ.004 p.m.

PLATE 120: Villa Brodu at Beuzeval (Calvados *département*); architect: Baumier.

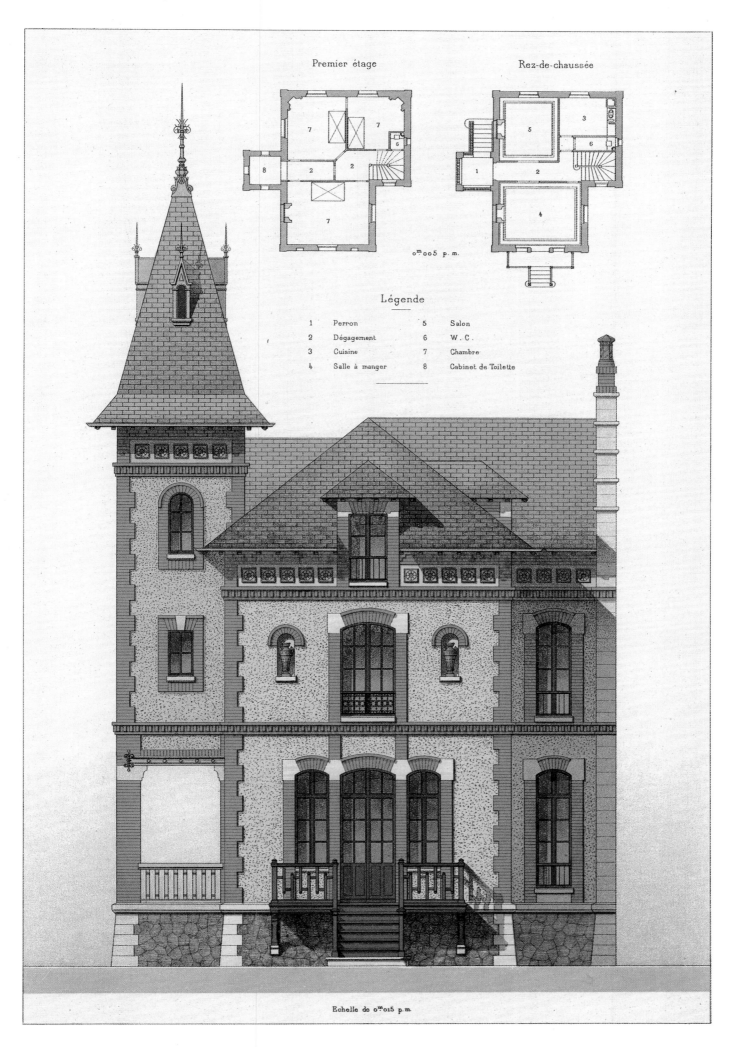

Premier étage   Rez-de-chaussée

0^m005 p.m.

Légende

1	Perron	5	Salon
2	Dégagement	6	W.C.
3	Cuisine	7	Chambre
4	Salle à manger	8	Cabinet de Toilette

Echelle de 0^m015 p.m.

PLATE 121: Villa at Villemomble (near Paris); architect: J. Amanovich.

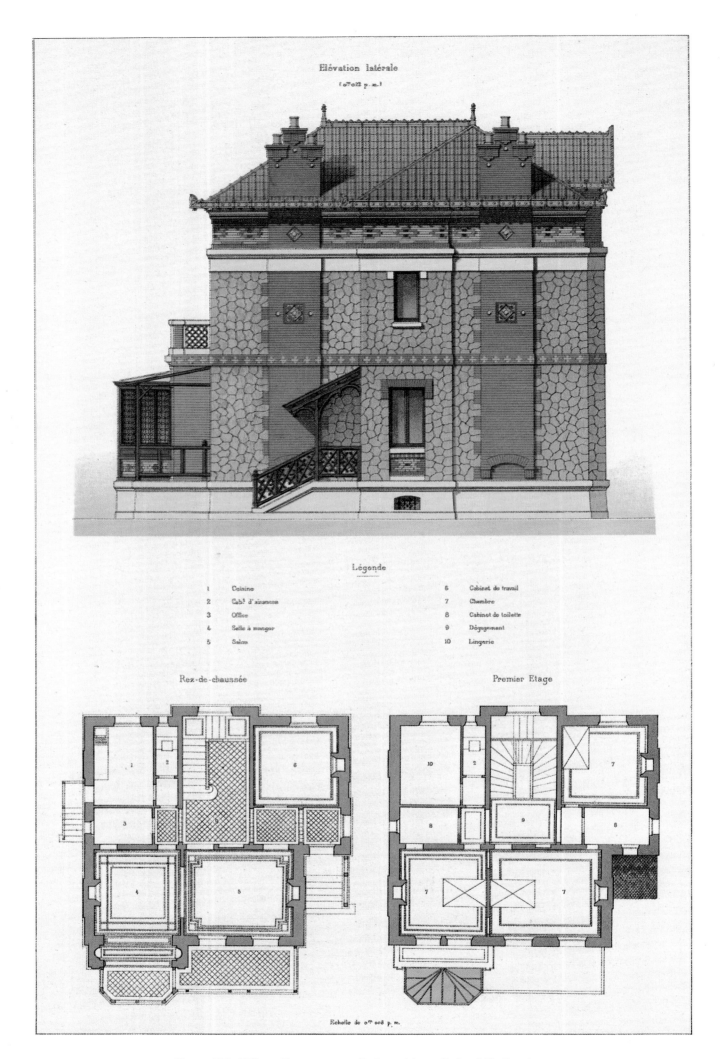

PLATE 122: Villa at Fontenay-sous-Bois; architect: E. Jandelle-Ramier.

Elévation Postérieure

Elévation Principale

Echelle de 0m015 p. m.

PLATE 123: Villa at Fontenay-sous-Bois; architect: E. Jandelle-Ramier.

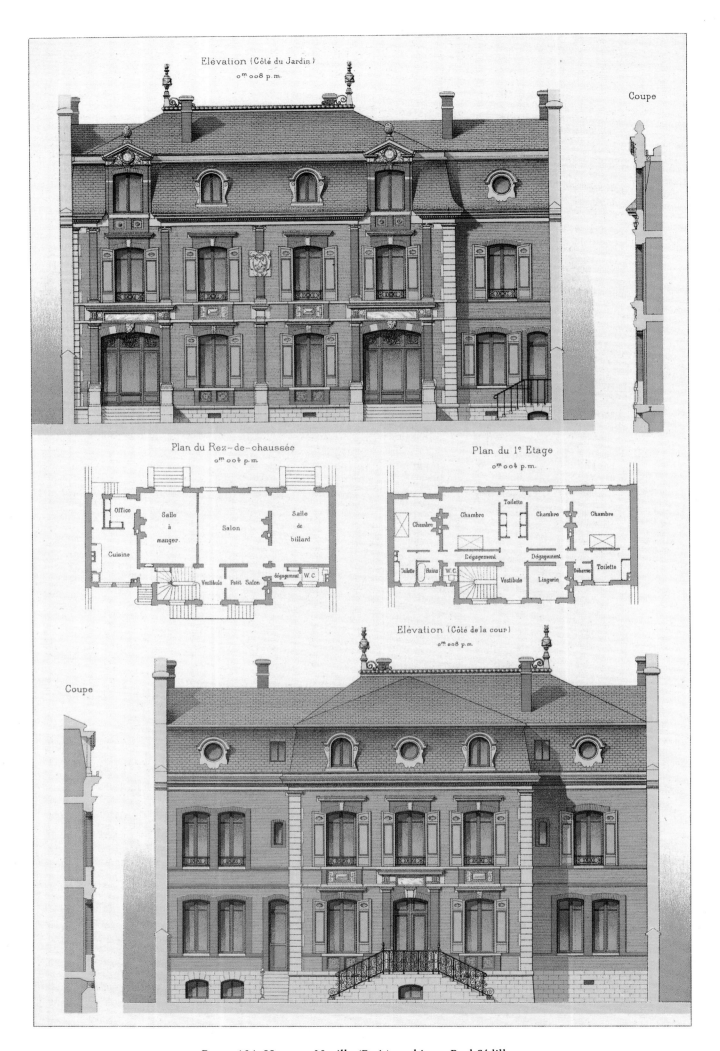

Elévation (Côté du Jardin)
0ᵐ008 p.m.

Coupe

Plan du Rez-de-chaussée
0ᵐ004 p.m.

Plan du 1ᵉ Étage
0ᵐ004 p.m.

Office

Salle à manger.

Salon

Salle de billard

Cuisine

Vestibule   Petit Salon   Dégagement   W.C.

Chambre   Chambre   Toilette   Chambre   Chambre

Toilette   Bains   W.C.   Dégagement   Dégagement   Débarras   Toilette

Vestibule   Lingerie

Elévation (Côté de la cour)
0ᵐ008 p.m.

Coupe

Coupe

PLATE 124: House at Neuilly (Paris); architect: Paul Sédille.

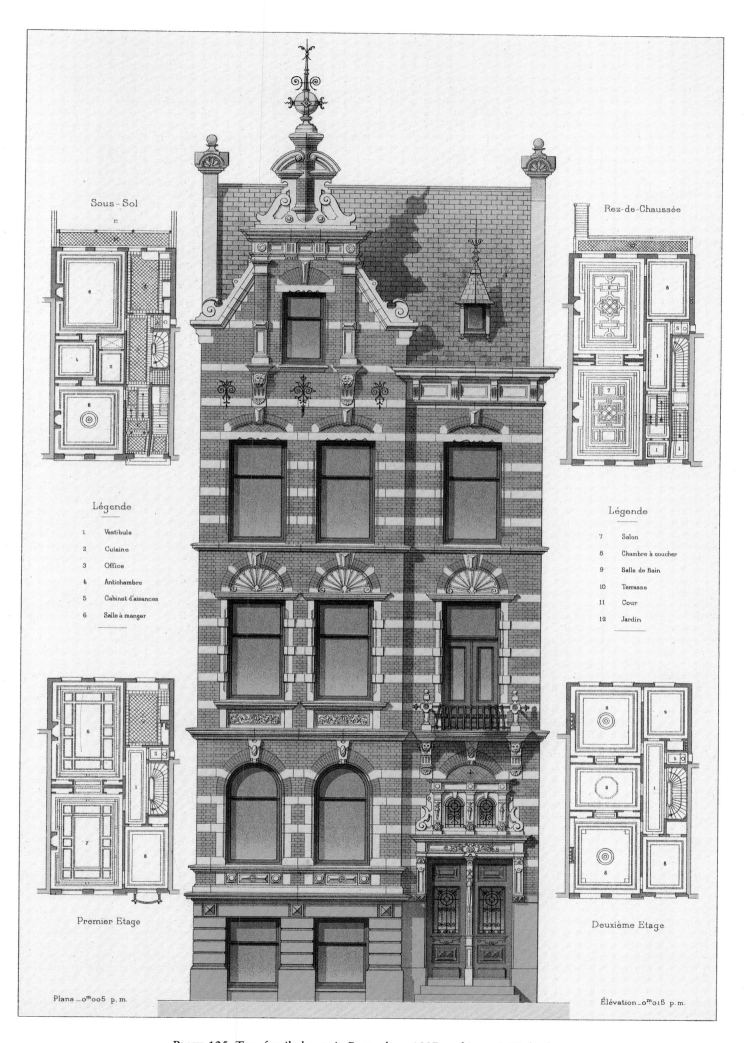

Sous-Sol

Rez-de-Chaussée

Légende

1   Vestibule
2   Cuisine
3   Office
4   Antichambre
5   Cabinet d'aisances
6   Salle à manger

Légende

7   Salon
8   Chambre à coucher
9   Salle de Bain
10   Terrasse
11   Cour
12   Jardin

Premier Etage

Deuxième Etage

Plans _0ᵐ005 p. m.

Élévation _0ᵐ015 p. m.

PLATE 125: Two-family house in Rotterdam, 1887; architect: J. Verheul.

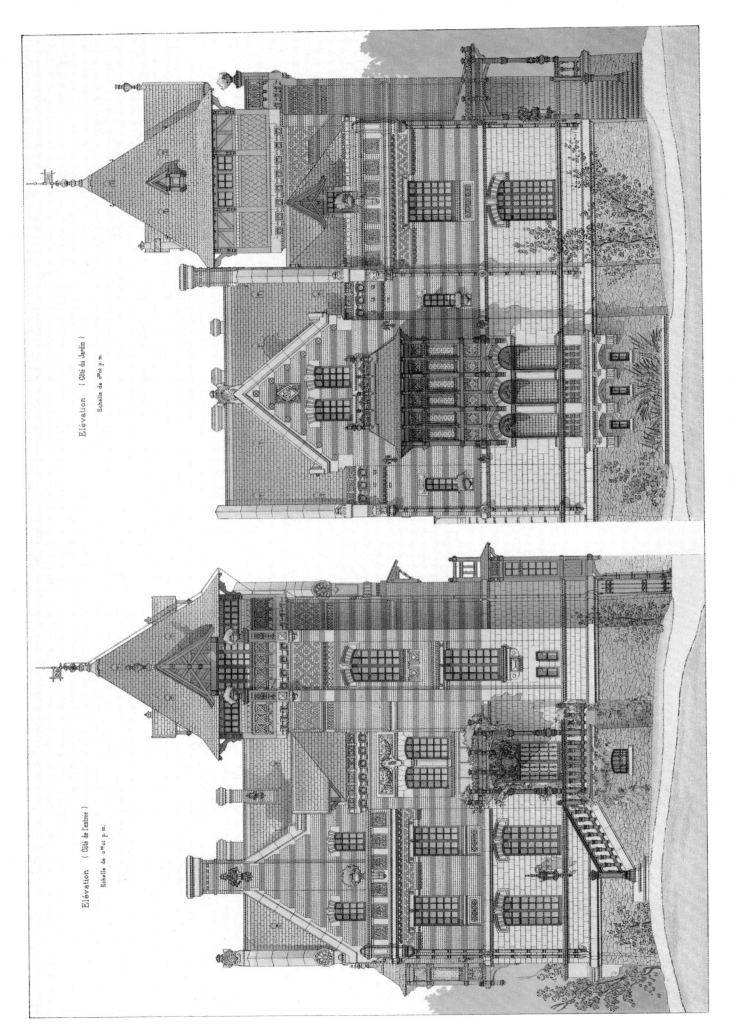

Elévation (Côté du Jardin)

Echelle de o^moi p. m.

Elévation (Côté de l'entrée)

Echelle de o^moi p. m.

PLATE 126: Competition design for a rural home; architect: Bonnier.

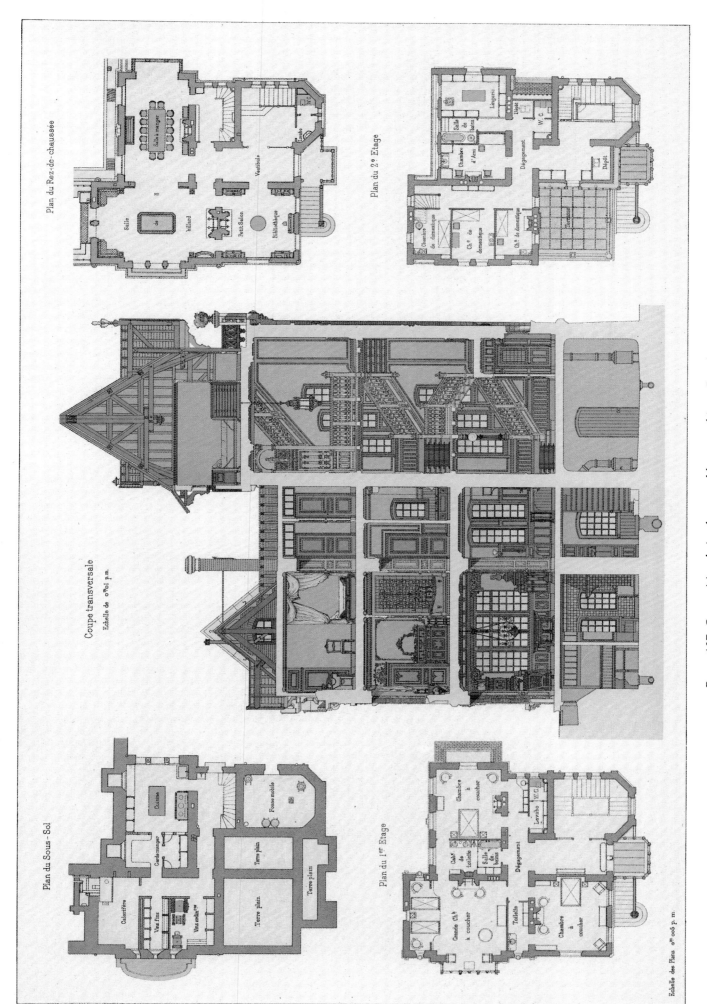

Plan du Rez-de-chaussée

Salle à manger

Vestibule

Salle de billard

Petit-Salon

Bibliothèque

W.C.

Plan du 2e Étage

Lingerie

Salle de bains

Chambre d'Ami

Dépôt

W.C.

Dégagement

Chambre de domestique

Ch.e de domestique

Ch.e de domestique

Terrasse

Dépôt

Coupe transversale

Echelle de o,o1 p.m.

Plan du Sous-Sol

Cuisine

Garde manger

Fosse mobile

Calorifère

Vins fins

Vins ordin.res

Terre plein

Terre plein

Terre plein

Terre plein

Plan du 1er Étage

Chambre à coucher

Salle de bains

Lavabo

W.C.

Cab.t de toilette

Dégagement

Grande Ch.re à coucher

Toilette

Chambre à coucher

Echelle des Plans o.m o05 p. m.

PLATE 127: Competition design for a rural home; architect: Bonnier.

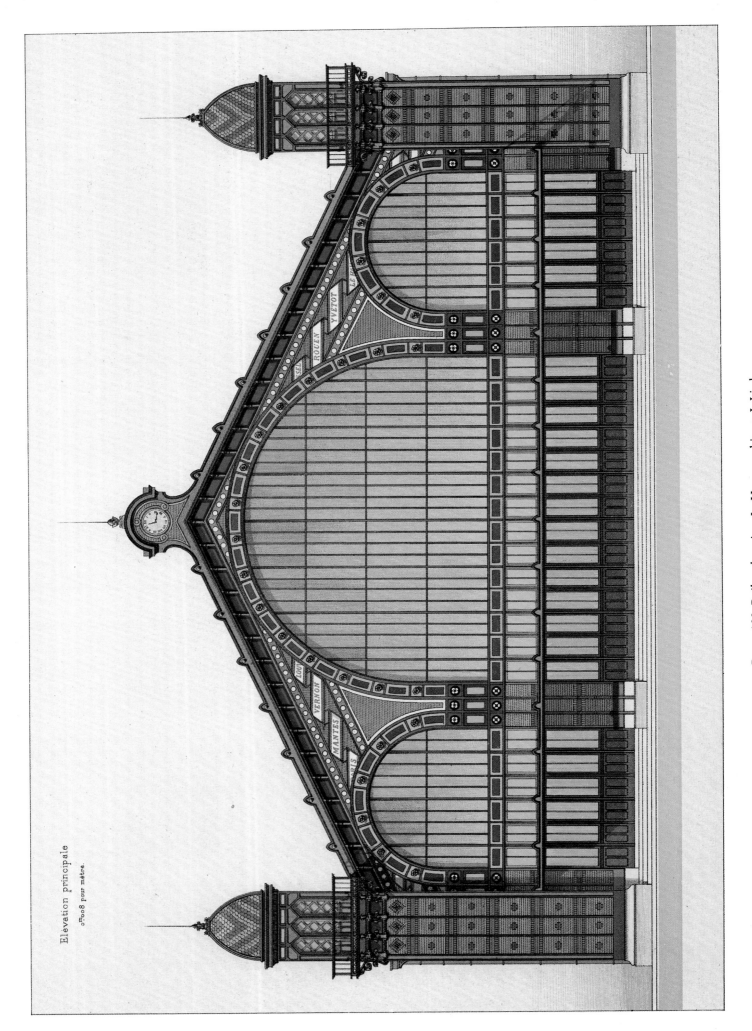

Élévation principale
0ᵐ008 pour mètre.

PLATE 128: Railroad station, Le Havre; architect: J. Lisch.

Coupe faite au dessous du balcon

Coupe sur les baies

Coupe du balcon

Coupe du chéneau

Echelle de 0.04 p. m.

PLATE 129: Pylon capping, Le Havre station; architect: J. Lisch.

Elévation _ o^m o1 p. m.

Plan _ o^m oo4 p. m.

Coupe

Face latérale

Chambre   W.C.   Cour   Cour   W.C.   Chambre

Office   Office

Salle à manger   Salle à manger

Salon   Salon

Côté de la mer

Echelle de o^m oo5 p. m.

PLATE 130: Villas at Trouville; architect: Jory.

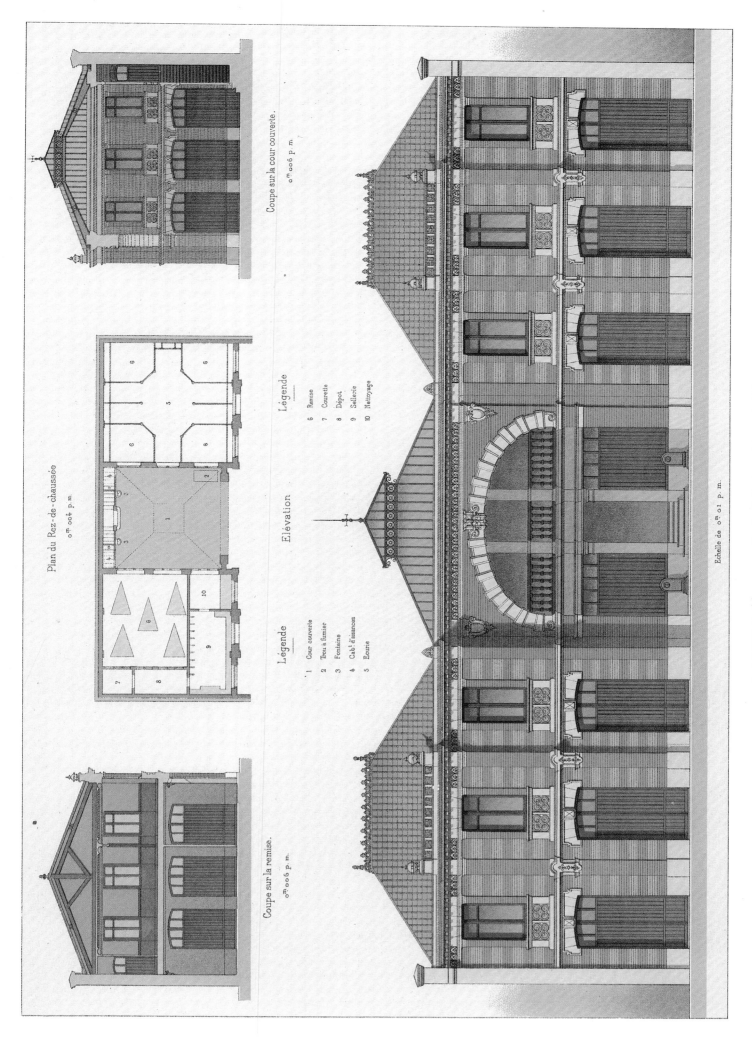

Plan du Rez-de-chaussée
0ᵐ·004 p. m.

Coupe sur la cour couverte.
0ᵐ·006 p. m.

Elévation

Coupe sur la remise.
0ᵐ·006 p. m.

Légende

1 Cour couverte
2 Trou à fumier
3 Fontaine
4 Cab.ᵗ d'aisances
5 Ecurie

Légende

6   Remise
7   Courette
8   Dépôt
9   Sellerie
10 Nettoyage

Echelle de 0ᵐ·01 p. m.

PLATE 131: Stables, avenue Raphaël, Paris; architect: A. Feine.

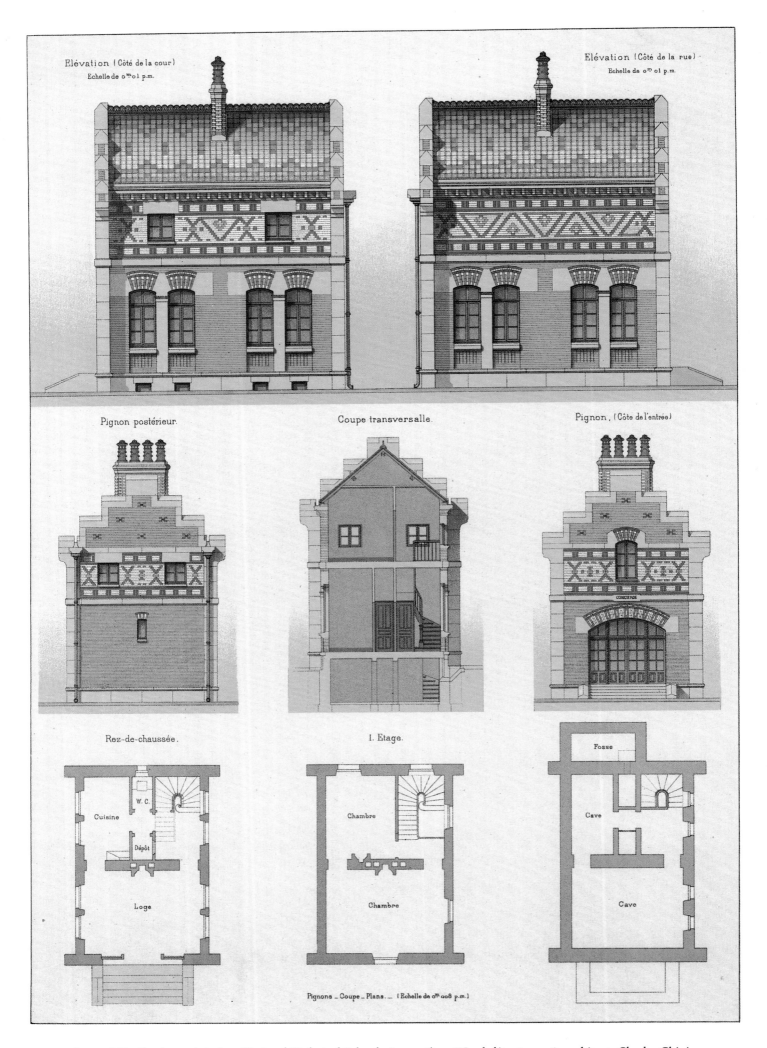

Elévation (Côté de la cour).
Echelle de o^m o1 p.m.

Elévation (Côté de la rue).
Echelle de o^m o1 p.m.

Pignon postérieur.

Coupe transversalle.

Pignon. (Côté de l'entrée).

CONCIERGE

Rez-de-chaussée.

Cuisine

W. C.

Dépôt

Loge

I. Etage.

Chambre

Chambre

Fosse

Cave

Cave

Pignons _ Coupe _ Plans _ (Echelle de o^m oo8 p.m.)

PLATE 132: Gatekeeper's lodge, National Technical School, Armentières (Nord *département*); architect: Charles Chipiez.

PLATE 133: Unrealized design for a villa at Cocqueville; architect: Robert de Massy.

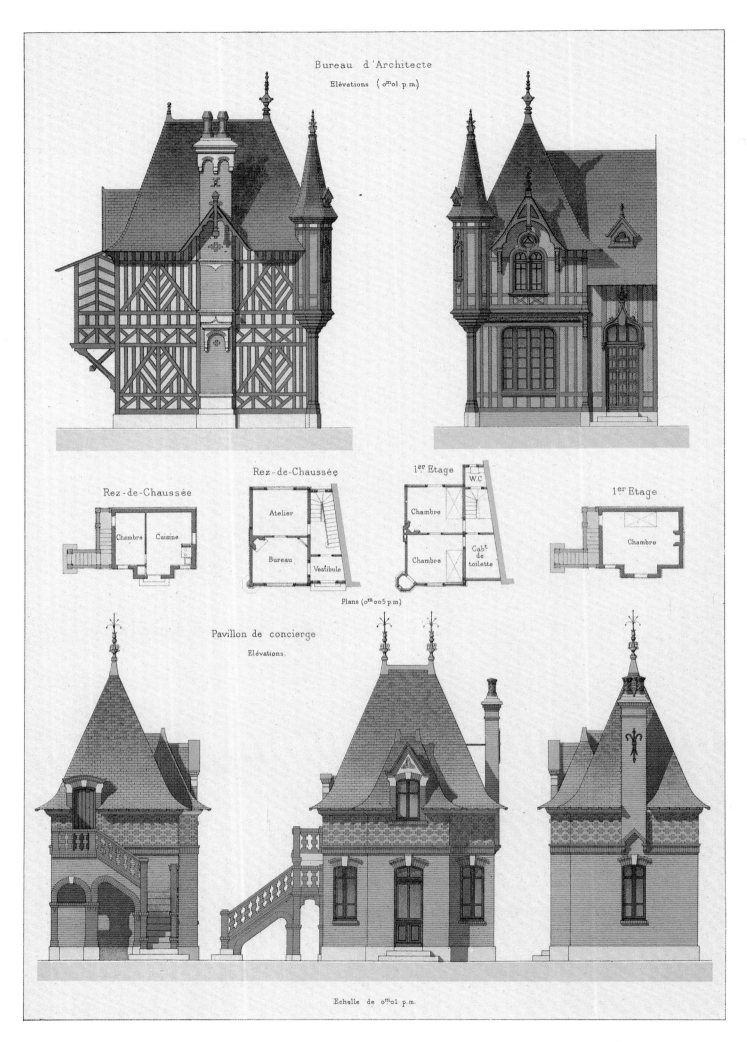

Bureau d'Architecte

Elévations (o^mo1 p.m)

Rez-de-Chaussée

Chambre   Cuisine

Rez-de-Chaussée

Atelier

Bureau   Vestibule

1er Etage

W.C

Chambre

Chambre   Cab^t de toilette

1er Etage

Chambre

Plans (o^moo5 p.m)

Pavillon de concierge

Elévations.

Echelle de o^mo1 p.m.

PLATE 134: Architect's office, Houlgate, and gatekeeper's lodge, Bénerville; architect: Edouard Lewicki.

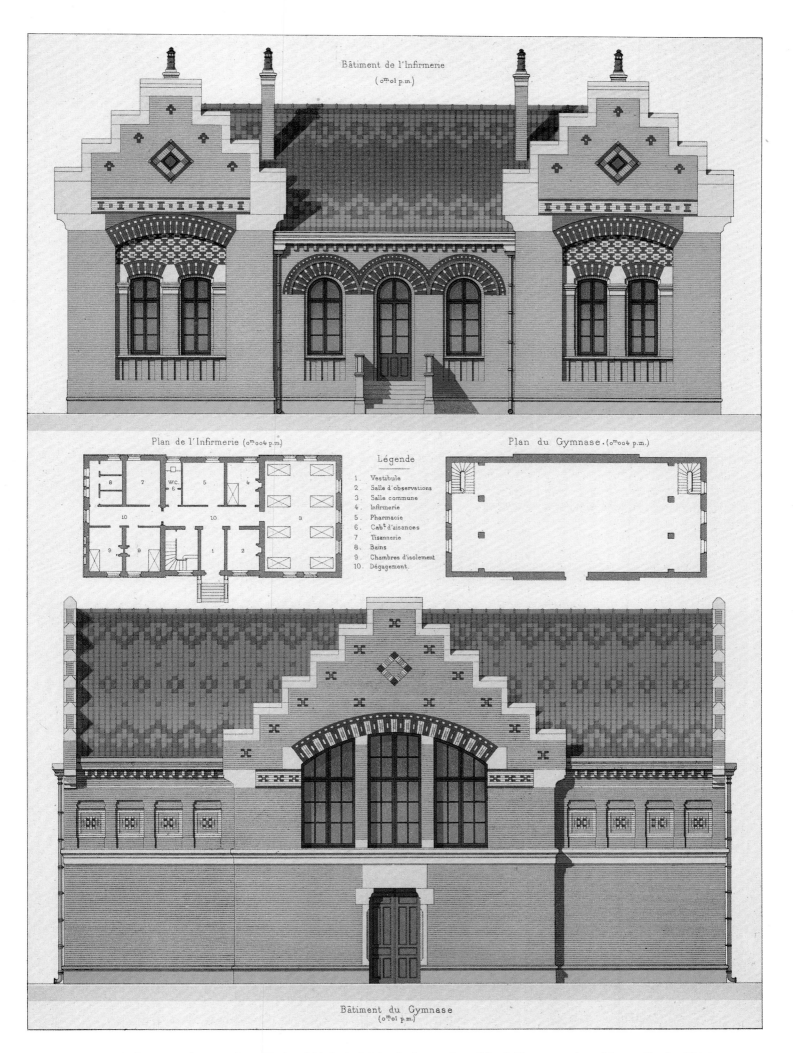

Bâtiment de l'Infirmerie
(0ᵐ01 p.m.)

Plan de l'Infirmerie (0ᵐ004 p.m.)

Plan du Gymnase. (0ᵐ004 p.m.)

Légende

1. Vestibule
2. Salle d'observations
3. Salle commune
4. Infirmerie
5. Pharmacie
6. Cabᵗ d'aisances
7. Tisannerie
8. Bains
9. Chambres d'isolement
10. Dégagement.

Bâtiment du Gymnase
(0ᵐ01 p.m.)

PLATE 135: Infirmary and gymnasium, National Technical School, Armentières (Nord *département*); architect: Charles Chipiez.

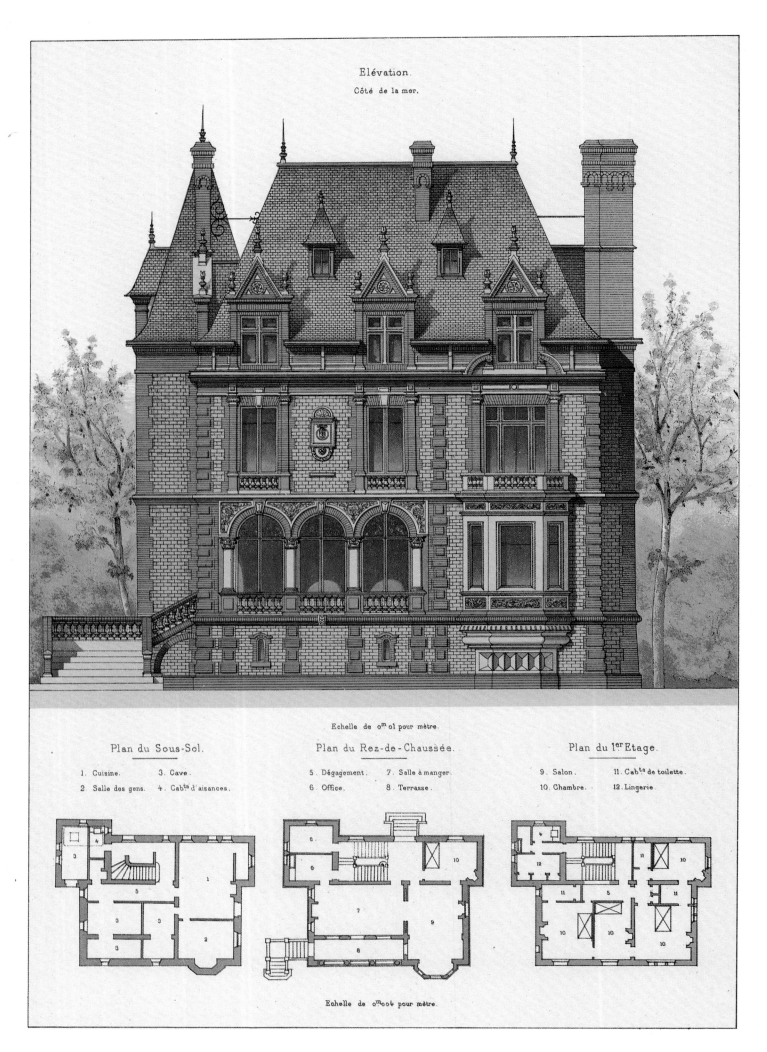

Elévation.

Côté de la mer.

Echelle de 0ᵐ 01 pour mètre.

Plan du Sous-Sol.

1. Cuisine.   3. Cave.
2. Salle des gens.   4. Cabᵗˢ d'aisances.

Plan du Rez-de-Chaussée.

5. Dégagement.   7. Salle à manger.
6. Office.   8. Terrasse.

Plan du 1ᵉʳ Étage.

9. Salon.   11. Cabᵗˢ de toilette.
10. Chambre.   12. Lingerie.

Echelle de 0ᵐ 004 pour mètre.

PLATE 136: Villa "La Salamandre" at Houlgate (near Deauville); architect: Baumier.

Plan des Caves

Vins
4, 20

Vins

Cave à bois

Buanderie

Fosse

Plan du Rez-de-chaussée

Salon

Salle à manger

P.t Salon

Plan des Combles

Chambre

Séchoir

Lingerie

Chambre

Plan du 1.er Etage

Chambre

Chambre

Antichambre

W.C.

Chambre

Bains

Coupe 0.m 005 p.m.

Echelle des Plans 0.m 004 p.m.

PLATE 137: Villa at Fontainebleau; architect: Brunnarius.

PLATE 138: Villas at Deauville; architects: H. Blondel (left) and Breney.

Echelle de 0ᵐ.01 p. m.

PLATE 139: Pavilion of the Great Tilery of (Montchanin,) Burgundy, 1889 fair; architects: Wulliam and Farges.

Détail
oᵐo4 p.m.

Plan oᵐoo5 p.m.

Echelle de oᵐ.oo5 p.m.

GRANDE TUILERIE DE BOURGOGNE
MONTCHANIN

PLATE 140: Pavilion of the Great Tilery of Burgundy, 1889 fair; architects: Wulliam and Farges.

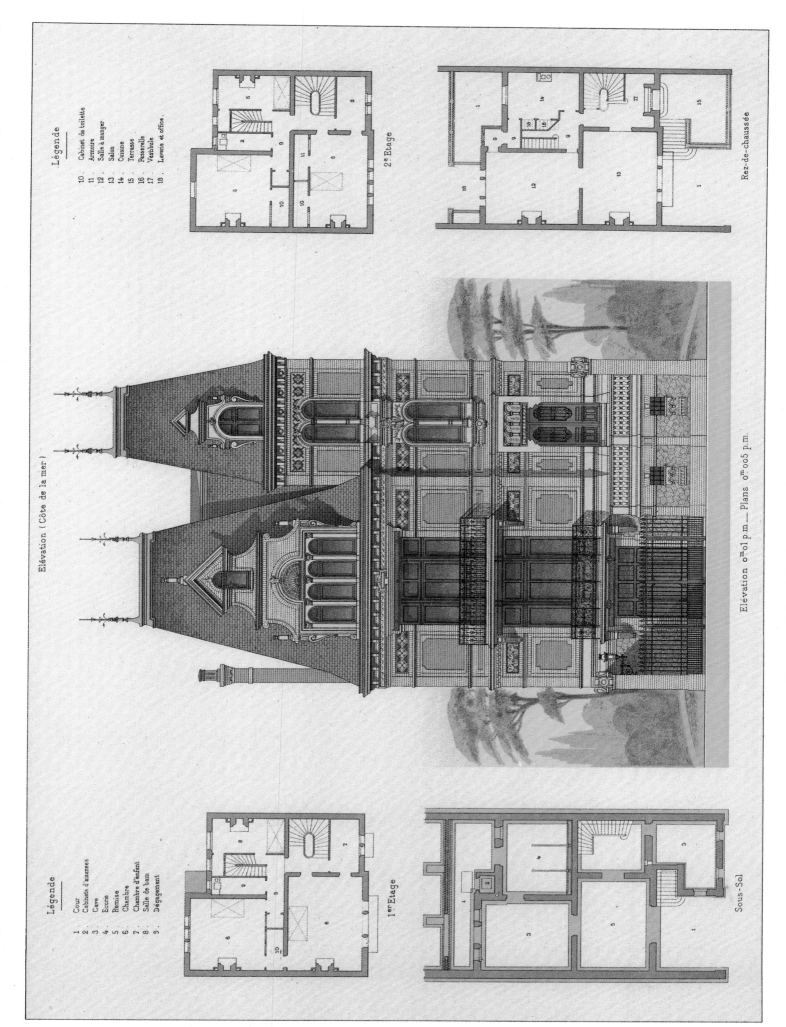

Elévation (Côte de la mer)

2.e Étage

1er Étage

Sous-Sol

Rez-de-chaussée

Elévation 0m·01 p.m. — Plans 0m·005 p.m.

PLATE 141: Villa "Adélaïde" at Trouville; architect: Delarue.

Elévation
0ᵐ015 p.m.

R·F.

PLATE 142: Staircase pavilion, National Technical School, Armentières (Nord *département*); architect: Charles Chipiez.

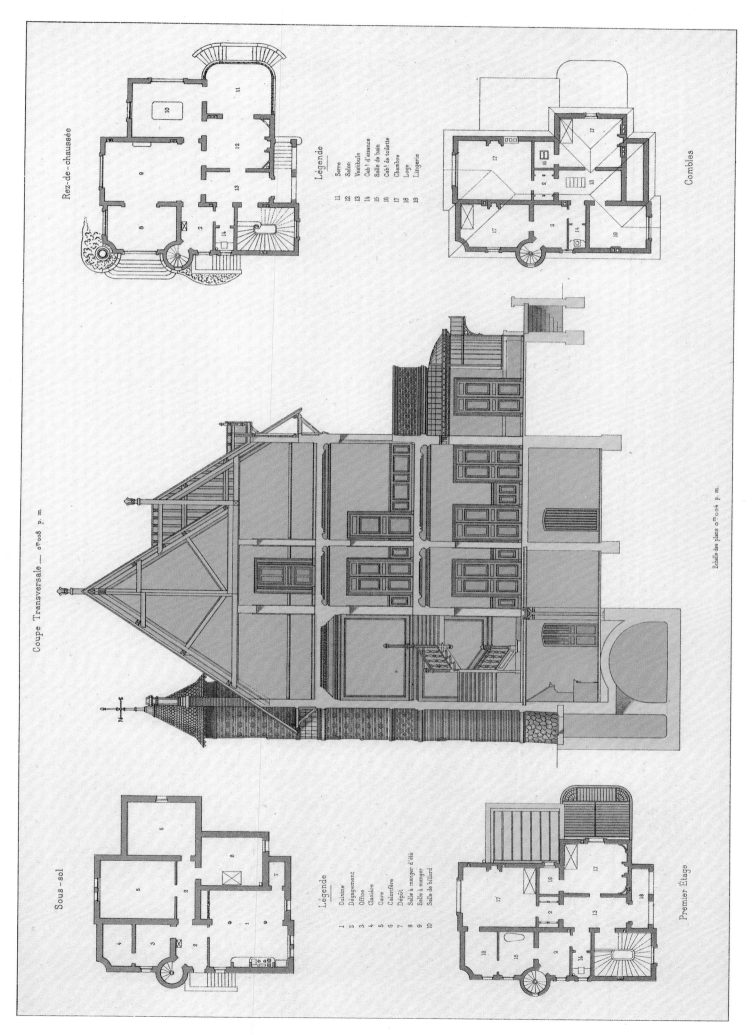

Coupe Transversale — o^m008 p. m.

Rez-de-chaussée

Combles

Légende

Serre
Salon
Vestibule
Cab.^t d'aisance
Salle de bain
Cab.^t de toilette
Chambre
Loge
Lingerie

11
12
13
14
15
16
17
18
19

Sous-sol

Légende

Cuisine
Dégagement
Office
Glacière
Cave
Calorifère
Dépôt
Salle à manger d'été
Salle à manger
Salle de billard

1
2
3
4
5
6
7
8
9
10

Premier Étage

Echelle des plans o^m004 p. m.

PLATE 143: Villa at Pont-à-Mousson (near Nancy); architect: Pierre Chabat.

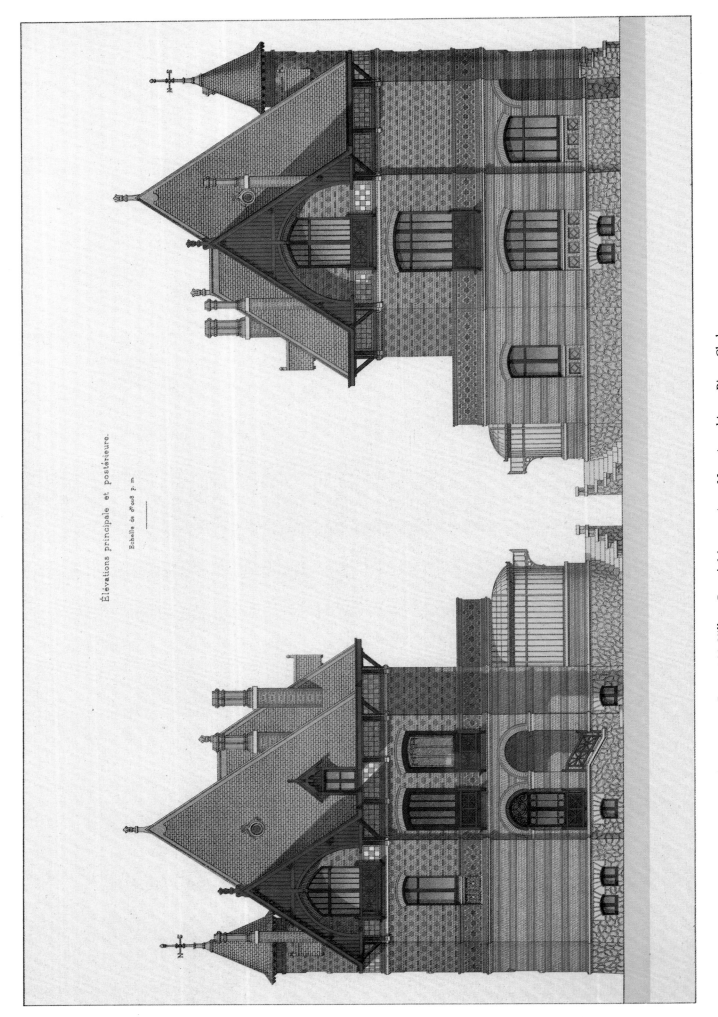

Élévations principale et postérieure.

Echelle de d'ous p. m.

PLATE 144: Villa at Pont-à-Mousson (near Nancy); architect: Pierre Chabat.

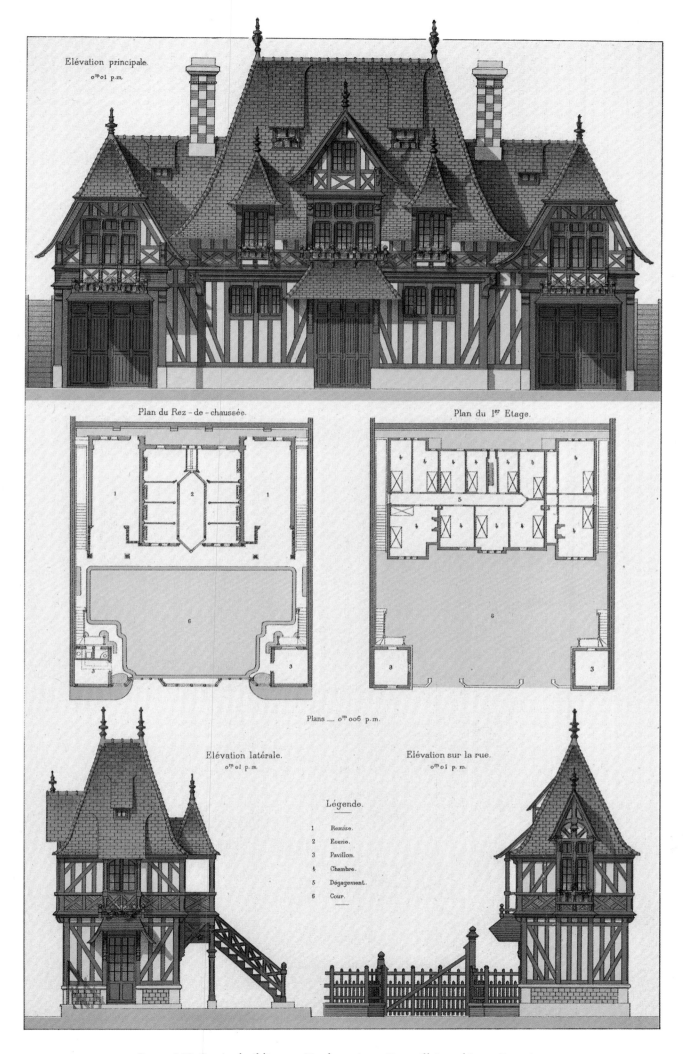

Elévation principale.
0ᵐ01 p.m.

Plan du Rez – de – chaussée.

Plan du 1ᵉʳ Etage.

Plans — 0ᵐ006 p.m.

Elévation latérale.
0ᵐ01 p.m.

Elévation sur la rue.
0ᵐ01 p.m.

Légende.

1   Remise.
2   Ecurie.
3   Pavillon.
4   Chambre.
5   Dégagement.
6   Cour.

PLATE 145: Service buildings at Houlgate (near Deauville); architect: Baumier.

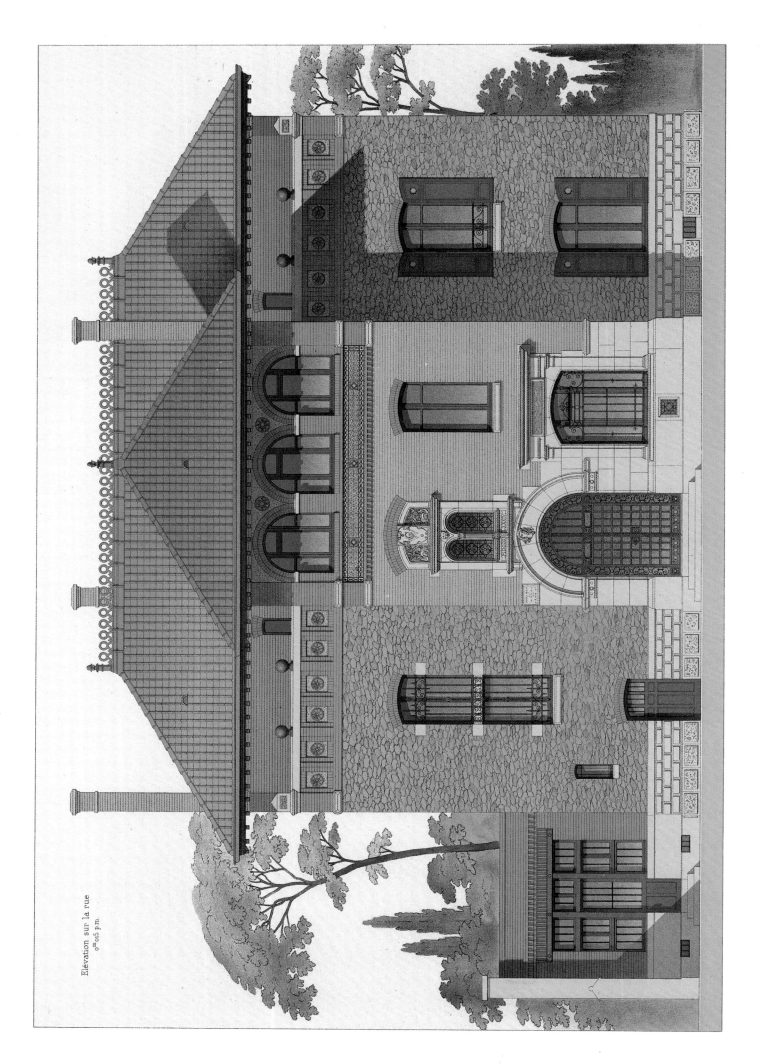

Elévation sur la rue
0ᵐ015 p.m.

PLATE 146: *Villa Weber, rue Erlanger, Paris; architect: Paul Sédille.*

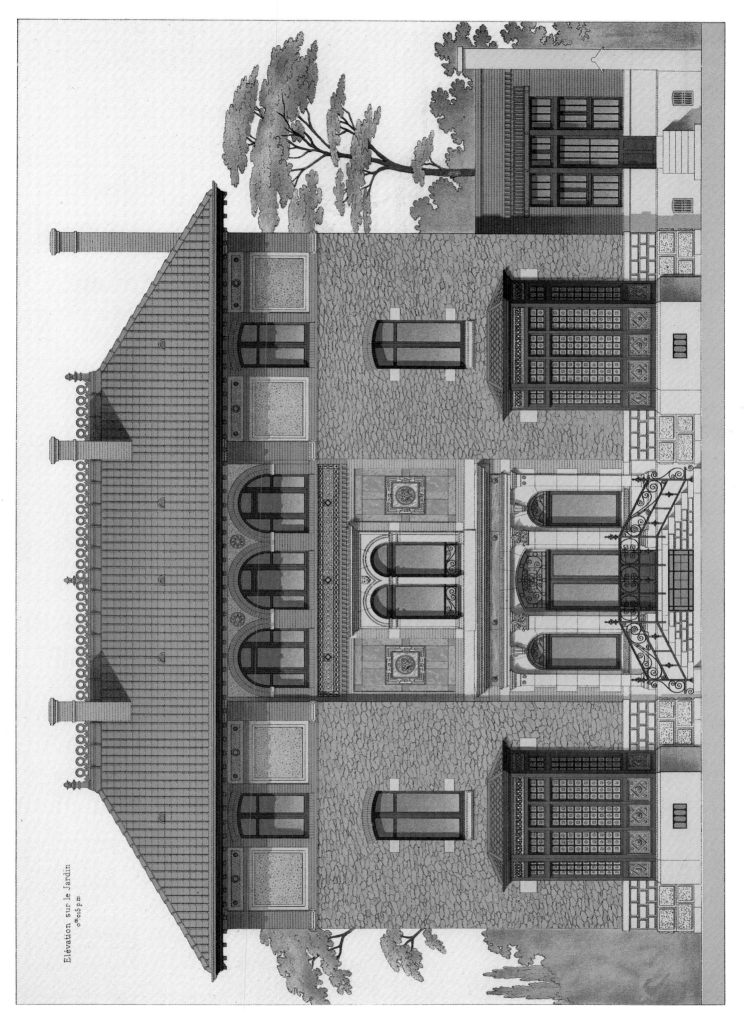

Elévation sur le Jardin
0ᵐ.0,5 p m

PLATE 147: Villa Weber, rue Erlanger, Paris; architect: Paul Sédille.

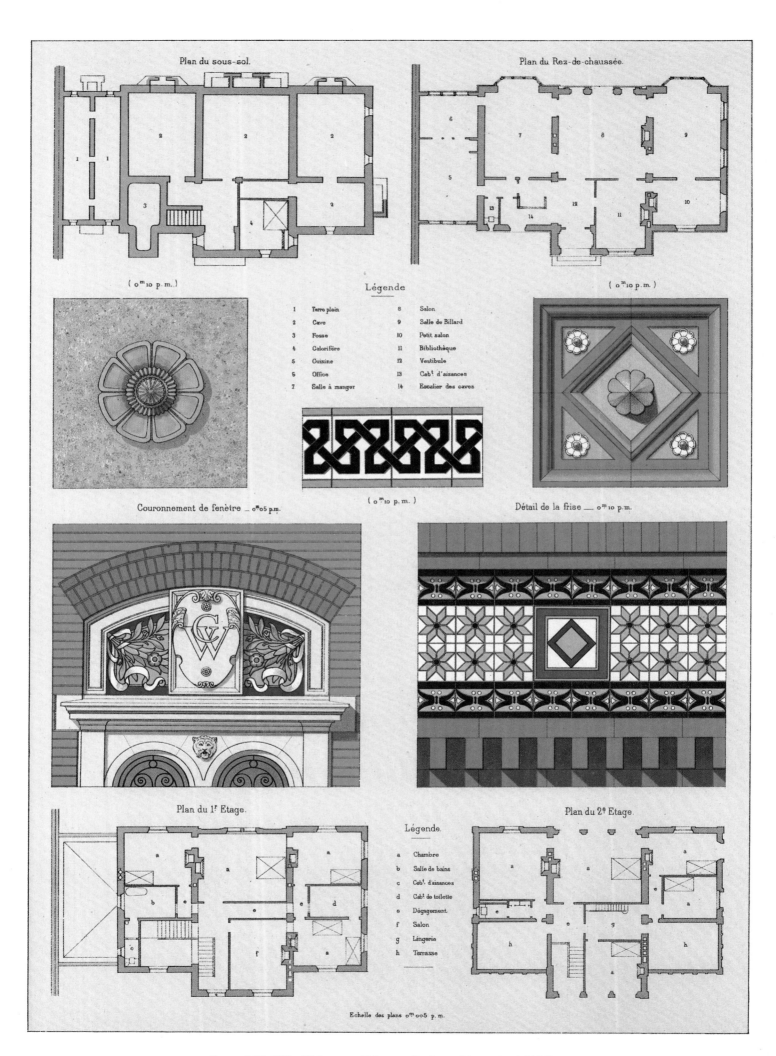

Plan du sous-sol.

(0ᵐ10 p.·m.)

Légende

1	Terre plein	8	Salon
2	Cave	9	Salle de Billard
3	Fosse	10	Petit salon
4	Calorifère	11	Bibliothèque
5	Cuisine	12	Vestibule
6	Office	13	Cabᵗ d'aisances
7	Salle à manger	14	Escalier des caves

Plan du Rez-de-chaussée.

(0ᵐ10 p.m.)

Couronnement de fenêtre — 0ᵐ05 p.m.

(0ᵐ10 p. m.)

Détail de la frise — 0ᵐ10 p.m.

Plan du 1ᵉ Etage.

Légende.

a	Chambre
b	Salle de bains
c	Cabᵗ d'aisances
d	Cabᵗ de toilette
e	Dégagement
f	Salon
g	Lingerie
h	Terrasse

Plan du 2ᵉ Etage.

Echelle des plans 0ᵐ005 p. m.

PLATE 148: Villa Weber, rue Erlanger, Paris; architect: Paul Sédille.

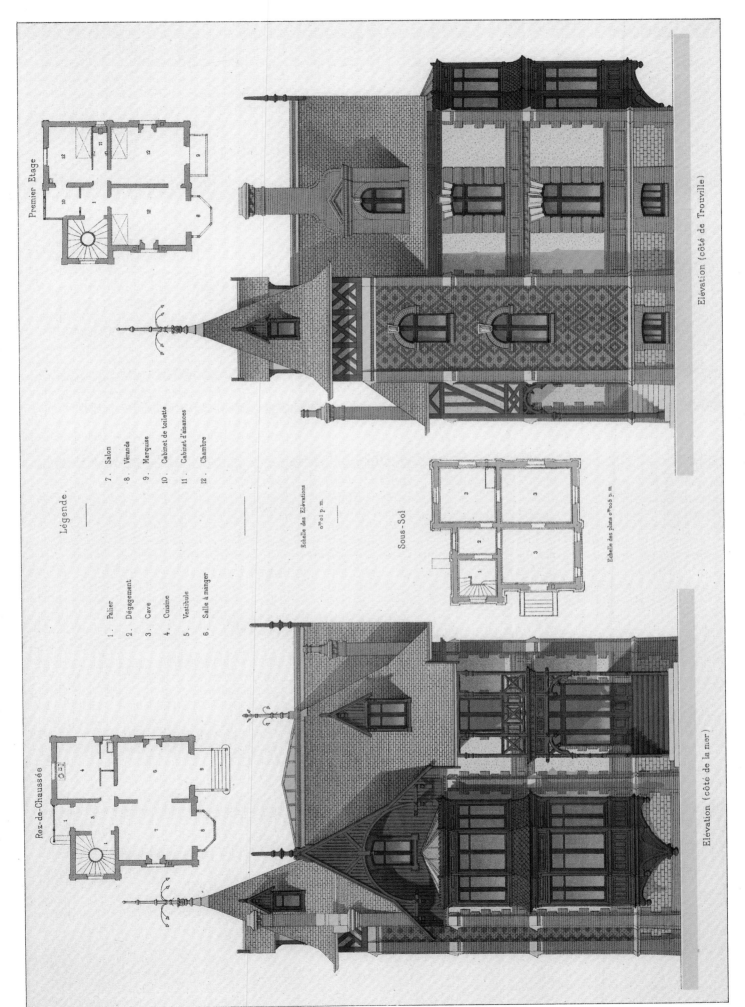

Premier Étage

Légende.

1.	Palier	7.	Salon
2.	Dégagement	8.	Véranda
3.	Cave	9.	Marquise
4.	Cuisine	10.	Cabinet de toilette
5.	Vestibule	11.	Cabinet d'aisances
6.	Salle à manger	12.	Chambre

Echelle des Elévations
0ᵐ01 p. m.

Sous-Sol

Echelle des plans 0ᵐ005 p. m.

Rez-de-Chaussée

Elévation (côté de la mer)

Elévation (côté de Trouville)

PLATE 149: Villa at Trouville; architect: Delarue.

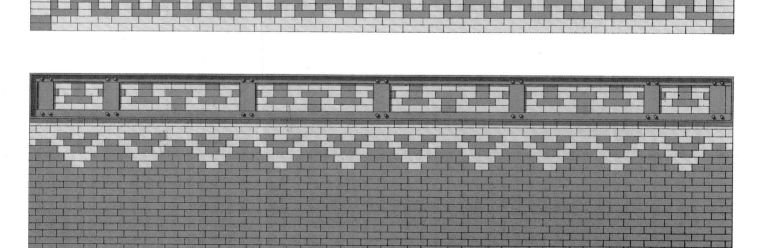

PLATE 150: Galerie des Machines, Exposition Universelle of 1889; architect: Ferdinand Dutert.

PLATE 151: Chimney shafts, from cities in France and Switzerland.

PLATE 152: Villa "La Hutte" at Deauville; architect: E. Saintin.

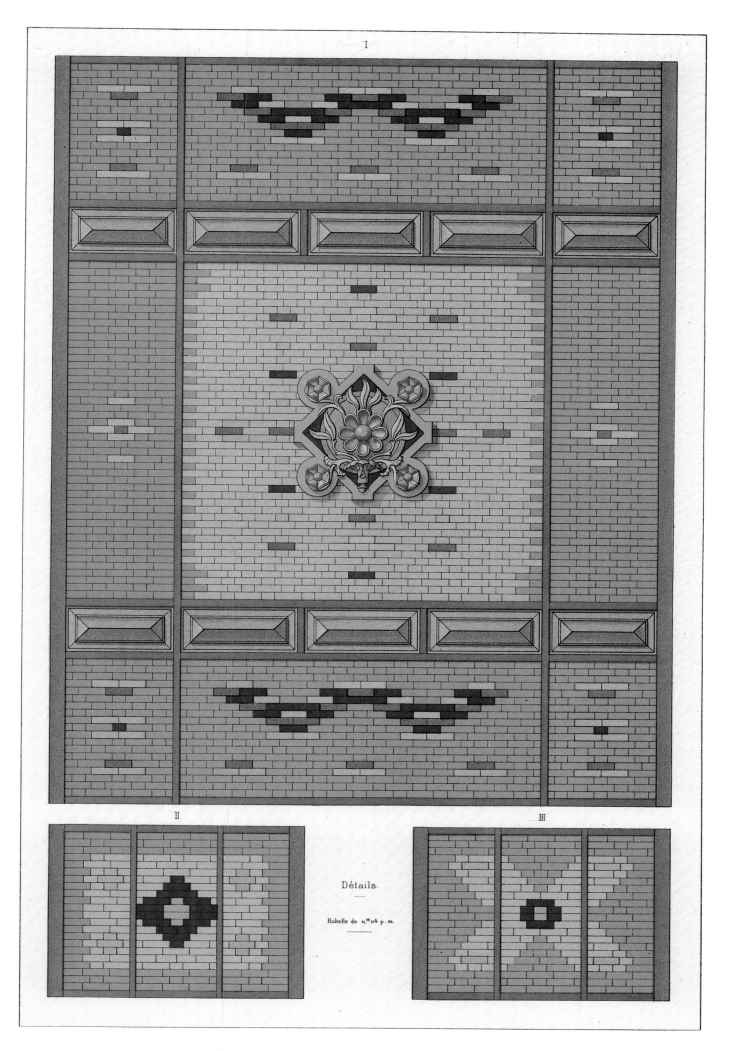

I

II III

Détails.

Echelle de 0.^m04 p. m.

PLATE 153: Central dome, Exposition Universelle of 1889; architect: J. Bouvard.

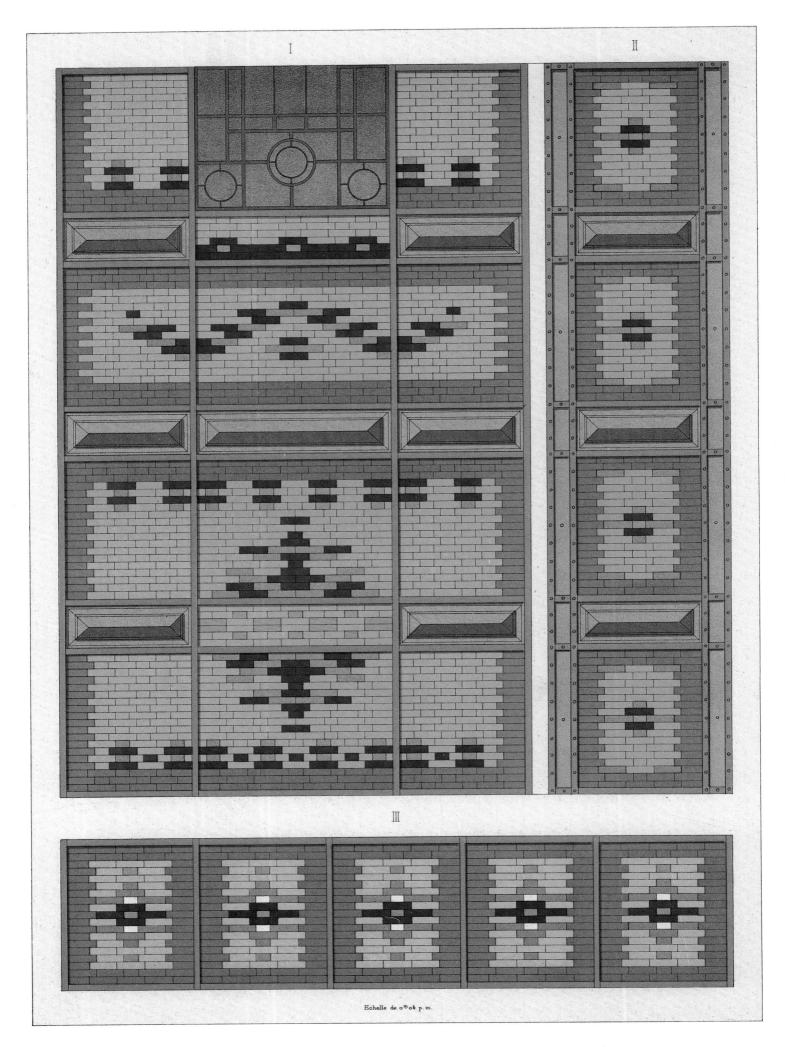

I

II

III

Echelle de 0ᵐ.04 p. m.

PLATE 154: Central dome, Exposition Universelle of 1889; architect: J. Bouvard.

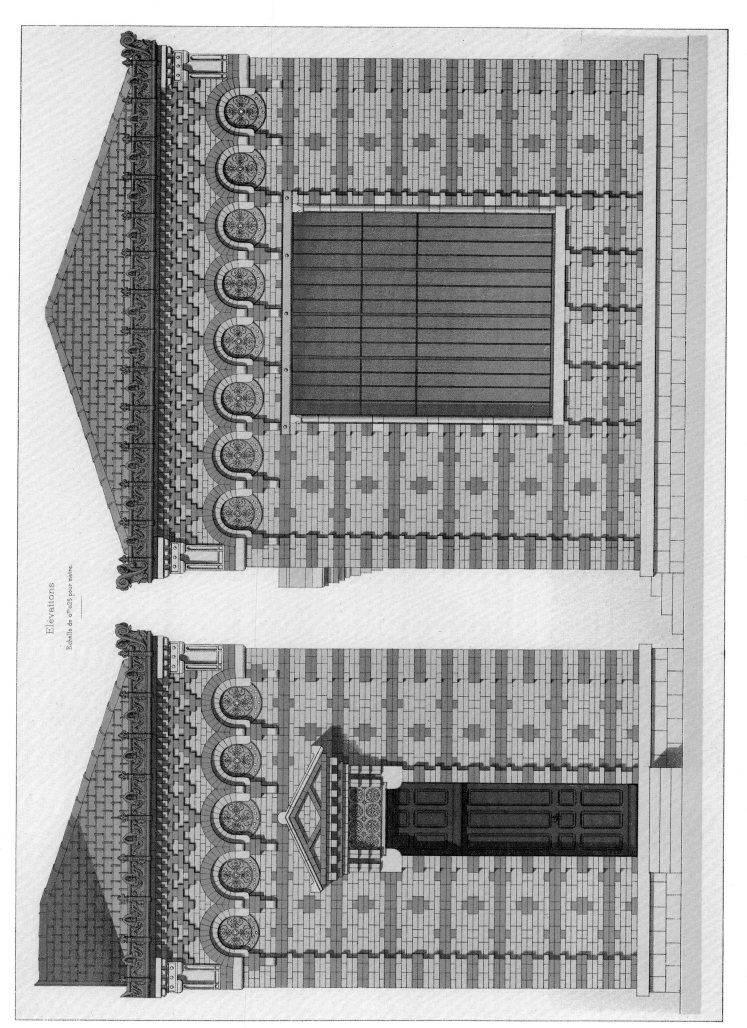

Elévations

Echelle de o^mo25 pour mètre.

PLATE 155: Painter's studio, Neuilly (Paris); architect: Simonet.

Elévation
(o . o15 p. m.)

Plan
o . o1 p. m.

Plan du comble
o . o1 p. m.

Coupe o . o15 p. m.

PLATE 156: Pavilion of the tile and brick firm Royaux *fils*, 1889 fair; architects: Pierre Chabat and E. Degand.

PLATE 157: Design for a seaside house; architect: Hügelin.

Echelle de 0ᵐ,03 p. m.

PLATE 158: Palace of Fine and Liberal Arts, 1889 world's fair; architect: Formigé.

Partie supérieure d'une travée.

Echelle de 0^m 02 p.m.

MANSARD
1646 – 1708

PLATE 159: Palace of Fine and Liberal Arts, 1889 world's fair; architect: Formigé.

PLATE 160: House, rue de la Faisanderie, Paris, architect: Scellier de Gisors.